HATFIELD
AND ITS PEOPLE

THE STORY OF A NEW TOWN, A GARDEN CITY,
AN OLD VILLAGE, A HISTORIC HOUSE, THE
FARMS AND THE COUNTRYSIDE
IN A HERTFORDSHIRE PARISH

CUMULATIVE INDEX

TO PARTS 1 – 12

by Hazel K. Bell

Published June 2015

Published by Hatfield Local History Society 2015
Printed on demand via www.lulu.com

Index – copyright © 2015 Hazel K. Bell

Edited by G. Philip Marris
Cover design by Henry W. Gray

All rights reserved. No part of this book may be reproduced or transmitted in any form or by any means, electronic or mechanical, including photocopying, recording, or by any information storage and retrieval system without the written permission of Hatfield Local History Society.

ISBN 978-0-9928416-4-5

COVER DESIGN

Top: A seventeenth-century Hertfordshire plough-team

Bottom: The Comet Hotel

FOREWORD

WHEN the *Hatfield and its People* series of booklets was published fifty years ago by the Hatfield Branch of the Workers' Educational Association, it was rightly regarded as an exceptionally authoritative and informative work. It has since remained unchallenged as the prime source of reference for anyone interested in the history of Hatfield.

Recognising its enduring value, members of Hatfield Local History Society reissued the series in 2014 with an index added to each of the twelve parts. These indexes have now been expanded and cumulated into one, with the aim of allowing greater access to the information held in the series.

Hatfield Local History Society hopes that the reappearance of the *Hatfield and its People* series, with the addition of this cumulative index, will encourage and stimulate others to undertake new research into Hatfield's past.

The *Workers' Educational Association,* founded in 1903, is a charity and the UK's largest voluntary sector provider of adult education, delivering 9,500 part-time courses for over 74,000 people each year in England and Scotland.

Hatfield Local History Society is an association of people interested in the history of Hatfield. The Society's aims and objectives are to encourage and undertake research into Hatfield's history, to produce publications and to provide a forum for the exchange of information on the history of the Hatfield area.

Please contact Hatfield Local History Society for further information about this publication.

CUMULATIVE INDEX

THIS is the cumulative index to the *Hatfield and its People* series of booklets. The list of titles is as follows:

Part 1	A Thousand Years of History
Part 2	The Story of Roe Green and South Hatfield
Part 3	Pubs and Publicans
Part 4	Newgate Street
Part 5	Roads and Railways
Part 6	Law and Disorder
Part 7	Churches
Part 8	Schools
Part 9	Farming Yesterday and Today
Part 10	Houses
Part 11A	Families and Trades (pages 1-48)
Part 11B	Families and Trades (pages 49-99)
Part 12	The Twentieth Century

In this index, references are given in the form, **[Part no]**.page(s), as in the following examples:

Abercrombie, Sir Patrick **[12]**.18-19

indicates pages 18-19 of Part 12 (The Twentieth Century)

alehouses **[3]**.4-5, 24; **[11]**.6, 24, 25, 27, 58

indicates pages 4-5 and 24 of Part 3 (Pubs and Publicans) and pages 6, 24, 25, 27 and 58 of Part 11 (Families and Trades)

Note: Page numbers in *italics* indicate illustrations or maps. Page numbers in **bold type** indicate main references to a topic.

Abbreviations used in the index are: OS for Ordnance Survey; WGC for Welwyn Garden City; WWI and WWII for World Wars I and II.

A

A. A. roadsign **[5]**.*29*
A.1 road *see* Barnet By-Pass
A.1000 road *see* Great North Road
Abbot, Robert **[7]**.10, 11
Abbots Ripton **[5]**.28
Abbott, John **[6]**.13
Abercrombie, Sir Patrick **[12]**.18-19
Aberdeen **[5]**.4, 26, 28

accidents
   rail **[5]**.4, 13, 27-9
   road **[5]**.29; **[8]**.25
acorns **[8]**.21
Act of Settlement *1660* **[6]**.14-15
Adam atte Hide **[1]**.21
Adam de Walton **[4]**.9

Addison family [3].10
 Addison, Jonas [3].10
 Addison, Mary [11].10
 Addison, Nicholas [11].10, 13
Adey and White [3].29
Adkins, John [7].21
advertisements in Part [6], [7], [8], [9], [11B], [12]
advowson [7].5
aerodrome *see* de Havilland Aircraft Company
Agreeable Historian, The (Simpson) [8].9
Agricultural Revolution [9].21, 23
Agricultural Show [8].17
agricultural workers [2].30
 see also farmers
agriculture *see* arable land; farming; farms
Ailward's tenement [1].21
Alcock, Bishop [3].11
Aldbury, Herts [6].*9*
Aldwick [1].*18*
Aldworth, Joseph [5].*31*
Aldykes (Alderwyke) [2].25
 field [2].10, *20*, 32
 houses [10].*cover*, 24-5, 30
 OS grid ref. [10].31
ale [3].6; [4].23
 assize of [2].12; [3]. 4-5; [6].5-6
alehouses [3].**4-5**, 24; [11].6, 24, 25, 27, 58
 licensing [6].13
 listed [3].**29-32**
 Newgate Street [4].23
 see also names
aletaster [3].5
Alexandra House [8].32
Alexandra, Princess [7].18; [12].22, 26
Alexandra, Queen [8].18; [12].6
All Saints church [7].20, *20*, 31
Allen family [3].24
 Allen, Elizabeth [8].23; [11].10
almsgiving [6].11

almshouses [5].13
Anabaptists [7].21
Anderson, H. C. [12].6
Andrews, Bartholomew [11].*12*, 25
Andrews, H. (headmaster) [8].32
Andrews, H. C.: *John Briant* [11].68
Angel family [11].54
Angel inn [3].13, 29; [9].*24*, 30; [11].61
Angus, Messrs. [8].32
animals
 farm stock [9].43-4
 see also cattle; sheep
 stealing [6].21, 22, 23
 stray [6].6-7
 tolls [1].11
 see also types
Anne, Queen [11].59
Annual Register 1758 [11].77
Anothoth house [7].28
Ansell, Philip [4].19
Anstey-ad-Castrum [4].12
antiques [11].22
Antrobus, Rev. J. K. [7].25
Antrobus, Rev. Jocelyn James [7].12, 14
 Some Memories of Bishops Hatfield and Its Past [3].23; [10].27
apartments [11].87
apothecaries [11].10, 24, 25, 79-80, 83, 88
apprentices [6].5, 13
arable land
 in Domesday Book [1].**26-7**
 16-17c. [9].9-10
 18c. [9].17
 19c. [9].28, 31, 32, 34
 20c. 46, 47
 enclosure [6].11
 Poor Law [6].11
 Roe Green [2].16
 see also farming
Arbon, Matthew [4].19
Arbuthnot, Fr. David [7].28, 29

Arcade [12].13
Arch, Samuel [11].19
Archaeological Journal [10].8
Archer family [11].13
  Archer, Francis James [11].10
  Archer, James [11].10, 38, 39
  Archer, John [11].69
  Archer, Sarah [11].69
archers [6].20
architects [7].18, 25; [9].43; [11].88; [12].22
architecture [10].5, 29-30
Arlesey [5].28
Arm and Sword public house [3].*8*, 19, 29
Arm and Sword Yard [10].21;[11].*12*, 32
  OS grid ref. [10].31
Armstrong, R. [12].6
Arnold, Dr. Thomas [7].21
Arnold, Thomas (indicted, *1790*) [6].17
Arris, Edward [11].69, 79
Arris, Dr. Thomas [11].79
Arthur Guinness, Son & Co. [3].22, 30
Arthur, Thomas [11].79
asbestos tiles [10].8
Ascot (Ascots) farm [9].5, 40, 43, 44
ashes [9].22
Ashwell [6].15
Ashworth, Mary [8].32
assart [2].4; [4].6-7, 16
Assize Rolls [2].14
Assizes [2].27; [3].5; [6].6, 19
  1826 [6].18-19
Association ... for Apprehending ... Felons ... [3].14
Association of Gentlemen, Farmers ... [6].21
Astrye, Thomas [6].19
Astwick [2].*28*; [7].18; [9].5, 6, 18, 19, 20, 29, 31, 32
Astwick Court [11].31

Astwick Lodge Farm [11].61
Astwick Manor [1].*6, 20*, 22, 24; [2].13; [3].14; [4].*26*; [10].9; [11].31
  OS grid ref. [10].31
Astwick Manor Farm [9].42, 43, 44, 45, 48
Atholl, Earls of *see* Strathbogie
Atkins, Marion [6].16
Atkins, Richard [11].25
Atkins, Thomas [6].17
Atkinson family [11].9, 14, 24, 25
  property owned by [11].*8*
Atkinson, John [11].10, 19, 83
Atkinson, Samuel [3].19, 29, 30; [11].10, 24, 25, 27, 83
Attimore (Otmore, Adam atte More) Farm [9].32
Attimore Hall [5].23; [9].41
auctioneer [11].88
Audrey de Bassingburn [1].22
Audrey, St. [11].4
Auncells [6].6
Austin family [3].26; [11].24
  Austin, James [8].10, 31
  Austin, Sarah [11].34
  Austin, Stephen [8].22
Avery, Sophia [8].12, 27-8
Avis, Thomas [11].64
axial-stack houses [10].*14, 16*, 17, 19-20
Aylesbury [9].40
Aymer de Valence, 2nd Earl of Pembroke [4].8-9
Ayot
  estate [9].7
  Poor Rate [9].19
Ayot St. Lawrence [11].54
Ayott St. Peters [6].15

B

Babington, James [8].31
Back Street *see* Church Street
Bacon, Sir Nicholas [4].12
Badcock, Mary [11].30

Baden (Bawden), John [3].31
Bagwell, Henry [7].10
"baffle entrance" [10].13
bailiffs [11].86
bakehouses [11].13, 43, 44
Baker, Jno. (blacksmith) [11].*12*
Baker, John (*c.1251*) [1].22; [6].19
Baker, John (Farrier-Major) [11].74
Baker, Walter [9].34
bakers [7].22; [11].10, 13, 14, 22,
    25, 26, 27, **33, 34, 35**,
    43-4, 87
Bakers Arms pub [3].*8*, 15, 18, 23,
    29, [11].44, 74
  OS grid ref. [10].31
Baker's of Hertford [3].30, 32
bakery [2].25; [11].22, 35
Baldock [3].7; [5].6, 7, 9; [11].27
Baldock family [11].66
Baldock Lane [5].7
Baldrey, M. (Inspector) [8].28
Balfour, Eustace [7].16
Ballance, Dr. [11].83
Bamford family [11].73-4
  Bamford, Elizabeth [11].73
  Bamford, John [11].74
  Bamford, Nathaniel [11].74
  Bamford, Thomas [11].5,73-4
  Bamford, William [11].74
banker [11].88
Banks, Thomas [11].80
Baptists [7].23-4, 31
Barbar, John [9].15-16
barbers [11].25, 29, 88
  prices [11].35
Barbers (Barbours) Lodge
    (Barberslodge) farm
    [1].*15*; [9].5, 9, *25*, 46,
    47; [11].61
barber-surgeons [11].11, 79-80
Barbour, John [9].5
Barclay Corsets [12].15
Barclays Bank [1].4, 10
Bardall, John [11].40

Bardolphs [9].14
Barker, John [6].16
Barker, William [3].32
Barkway [7].24
barley
  for brewers [3].5; [11].36
  crops [9].17, 20, 21, 22, 24, 40,
    41, 47
  in diet [12].14
  transport [5].7
Barley, M. W. [10].13
Barley Weak field [2].19
Barn Mead bungalow [2].14
Barn Theatre [9].41
Barnes, Jeremiah [4].18
Barnes family [11].74
Barnet [3].24; [11].80
  railway [5].*11*, 19, *22*
Barnet by-pass (A.1) [1].4; [2].*6*,
    14, 17; [3].14, 31; [5].6,
    29; [6].15, 25; [9].14;
    [10].7; [11].66, 74;
    [12].13, 18
barns [1].*18*
Barns, William [11].27
Baron, James [4].19
Barrelegs, William [4].24
Bartelett (constable) [6].21
Bartelot, Thomas [11].13
Bartholomew de Barre [1].21, 22
Barton (forester) [9].45
Baseley, William [10].7
Basill, Fred [8].21
Basill, John [8].21
Basily family [2].24
basket maker [11].*12*, 86
Basset, Alice [6].6
Bassil, James, school [8].*30*, 31
Bassill family [3].21, 29; [11].43,
    [11].54, 55-8
  pedigree [11].*56*
Bassill, Alice [11].56
Bassill, Edward [11].56, 57
Bassill, Elizabeth [11].56

Bassill, Frederick [11].58
Bassill, George (*b.1631*) [11].56, 57
Bassill, George (*d.1670-1*) [11].56, 57
Bassill, George (*b.1770*) [11].56, 58
Bassill, George (*d.1770*) [11].56, 57-8
Bassill, George (*d.1786*) [11].56, 58
Bassill, James [11].65
Bassill, John [11].56, 58, 65
Bassill, Martha [11].56
Bassill, Mary [11].56
Bassill, Robert Smyth [11].56, 57
Bassill, Samuel [11].56
Bassill, Sarah [11].56
Bassill, Symon [11].55, 56, 57, 58
Bassill, Thomas [11].56
Bassill, William [11].56, 58
Bassills Field [11].58
Bassingbourn, Cambridgeshire [1].22
Bassingburn family [1].22
bastards [6].17
Bateman, John [11].63
Bateman, William [11].63
Batley, Henry [3].23
Battell family [9].41; [11].59-60
  Battell, Affabel [11].59
  Battell, Humphrey [11].59
  Battell, John [11].59
  Battell, Mary [9].10; [11].59
  Battell, Robert [11].59
  Battell, Sarah [11].16
  Battell, William [11].16, 59
Batterdale (Batterdell, Batterdelph) [2].30; [6].6, 20; [11].*8, 12*, 31, 33
  Malting [11].36-8
  Militia Barracks [8].17; [11].74
  pubs [3].*8*, 18, 31
  and rectory [7].9
  school [3].30; [8].31

tanning [11].38-40
Triangle House [8].*30*, 31; [10].19-20, 28; [11].39, 83
  OS grid ref. [10].32
Batterdale House (Colonel's House) [10].20-1; [11].3, *8*, 37-8, *37*, 66
  OS grid ref. [10].31
Batterdale Pond [1].*18*
Bayden, Ann [11].16
Bayford [4].8-9, 12, 13
Bayford Manor [4].10
Bazley, Sir Thomas [4].20
Beach family [11].54
Beaconsfield Road cottages [10].8, 24
  OS grid ref. [10].31
Beadles [6].22
Bean, Henry [11].63
beans [9].21
Beard, William [11].*12*, 15, 19, 29
Beasney (Bestney) family [9].41; [11].28-9
  Beasney, Elizabeth [11].16
  Beasney, James [11].*12*, 16, 29, 39
  Beasney, John [11].16, 28, 29
  Beasney, Thomas [11].*12*, 16, 28
Beaumont, Katherine [4].9
bedehouses [3].11
Bedford [5].18
Bedwell [4].*26*; [10].7
  OS grid ref. [10].31
Bedwell Louths [4].17
Bedwell Manor [1].*15, 20*; [11].9, 59
Beecroft, Charles [3].24; [6].21
Beehive pub [3].*17*, 21, 29; [9].*cover*, 30; [10].17
  OS grid ref. [10].31
  plan [10].*14*
beer [3].6
beer-houses [3].**15-22**, *32*; [4].23
  see also ale-houses; brewing

7

beggars [6].11, 14; [7].15
Belcher, Robert [6].16
Belgae [1].26
Belgic settlements [1].*25*, 26; [2].4
Bell Bar [1].4, *6*, 9, 11, *13*, *15*, 21-2;
    [5].8; [9].*24-5*; [11].8,
    59
  and G.N.R. [5].13
  inns [3].9, 27
Bell Inn [3].14, 31
Bellis, James [11].81
bells [11].66-8, *68*
Bene, Richard [11].63
Bennet, Benjamin [3].31
Bennett, George [4].24
Bennett, Richard [6].16
Bennett, Sarah [8].23
Benskins Brewery [3].6, 7, 14, 29,
    30, 31, 32
Berkhamstead [4].10, 13
Bernal, J. D. [9].48
Bernard the potter [10].6; [11].63
Berne, John [2].20; [3].5
Berner family [3].9
Berner, William [3].31
Berry, Mary [11].56
bespoke tailoring [11].22
Bettesworth, O. [4].3
Betts, William [7].10
Bibby, James [11].29
Bibles [11].62
bigamy [6].17
Bigg family [3].30
  Bigg, Anthony [11].60
  Bigg, Edward [11].60
  Bigg, Freeman [3].20, [11].60
  Bigg, John [3].10; [9].12; [11].10
  Bigg, Joseph [3].7; [11].11;
    [11].61, *65*
  Bigg (later Powell), Mary [11].22,
    61, 70
  Bigg, Richard [11].60
  Bigg, William [3].10, 30; [11].60
Bigge family [2].24
  Bigge, John [2].24

Bigge field [2].10
Biggleswade [5].6, 7, 27
  railway [5].*11*
Biggs family [11].60-2
  Biggs, Eliza, school [8].*30*, 31
Billock, John [6].19
Birch Field [1].*14*
Birch Wood (Birchwood) [1].*14*;
    [9].*24*
Birchwood estate
  churches [7].20, 27, *27*, 30, 31
  pub [3].20
Birchwood Farm [1].*14*; [3].23, 24;
    [9].17, 18, 20, 21, *24*,
    32, 38-9, *39*, 45;
    [11].61, 62
Birchwood field [1].17; [9].9, 13
Birchwood Nursery school [8].32
Bird, Rev. John Cox [7].24
Bird, Rev. Samuel [7].24
Birmingham [5].9
Bishop of London [8].4
Bishop's Hatfield parish [7].5, 10,
    14, 15
  see also Hatfield parish
Bishop's Hatfield "town" [11].38
bishops, Celtic missionary [7].5
Bishops of Ely [1].16, 18-19, 20;
    [2].8, 32; [4].6, 8, 10,
    16; [5].6; [6].7; [7].5, 7;
    [9].6; [10].6, 7; [11].4,
    46
  John Morton [1].19; [7].7;
    [10].7
Bishop's Palace *see* Old Palace
Bishops Rise [2].*6*, 32; [3].29, 30;
    [7].29
Bishops Stortford [5].9, *10*; [6].27;
    [9].40
Bishops Wood [8].32
Black Bull [3].*16*, 20, 29; [5].13
Black Death [1].19-20; [2].8, 24;
    [5].4
Blackland field [1].*14*, 17; [9].9

blacksmiths [4].5, 22; [11].*12*, 73-4
   forge [4].*22*
Blathroe, Henry [6].15
Blessed Philip Howard School
   [7].29; [8].32
Blessed Sacrament and St. Theresa
   [7].*27*, 29, 31
Bligh family [11].43, 54
   Bligh, George [3].29, [11].43
   Bligh, John [3].21, 29; [11].43
Blood an' Gut Alley [3].20
Blount, Elizabeth [4].17
Blount, William, Lord Mountjoy
   [4].17
Blountes Manor [4].17
Blue Bell [3].29
Blue Streak rocket [12].18
Boar and Castle pub [3].*17*, 21, 29;
   [5].8
Board of Agriculture [9].39
Board of Education [8].14, 15
Board of Guardians [11].46
Board of Trade [5].16
Board Schools [8].20
boarding school [4].5; [11].25
Boer War [8].18; [12].5, 7
Bokenhamhide (Bokymwykhide,
   Buckhamwykhyde,
   Bukhamwik,
   Bukhamwyk)
   see Woodside
Bolter's Cottage [10].20
   OS grid ref. [10].31
bomb damage
   1940 [12].17
   1944 [6].26; [8].15
Bone, Ambrose [3].13
Bookham parish, Surrey [4].19
boots [11].22
Bosanquet, Peter [7].18
Bosford, William [11].64
Boston [5].14
"Botany Bay" [1].7
Boteler family [3].19; [5].13; [9].7
   Boteler, Sir Henry [6].10

Boteler, Sir Philip [6].10
Bottomley (née Houghton), Mrs. B.
   [8].13, 29
boundary dispute [2].23
Bourchier, Henry, Earl of Essex
   [4].17
Bourne, Cardinal Archbishop
   [7].28-9
Bovingdon Chapelry [1].5
Bowne, Hy [11].*12*
Bowstyle [6].7
Boyd, Kenneth [7].18
Bracey family [11].54
   Bracey (railway employee)
   [11].40
Bracy (poacher) [6].19
Bradbeer, Frank [10].8
Bradbury, Sarah [8].23
Braddock, R. [8].32
Bradshaw family [3].18, 21
   Bradshaw, Charles [3].7, 8
   Bradshaw, George [3].7, 8, 29;
   [11].13
   Bradshaw, John [3].31
Bradshaw's Brewery [2].32; [3].*17*,
   31, 32; [7].31
Bradshaw's Railway Guide [5].19,
   21, *22*
Brain, Dennis [5].29
Brambles cottage [2].31
Bramfield [3].6, 14
Branch Johnson, W. [5].7
Brandon, David [7].16
Brassey, Mr. (of railway
   construction) [5].12
Bray family [2].30
Brazilian Hats [2].30
breach of promise [11].15
bread
   assizes [6].5
   at church door [7].13, 14-15
   as legacy [11].13
   see also bakers; bakery
breeches-maker [11].*12*, 40, 87
Brethren [7].18, 31

Brett, Lionel [7].18; [12].21-2, 25
Brewer, Thomas [3].5
breweries [1].10; [3].5-9, 29, 30
   Benskins [3].6, 7, 14, 29, 30, 31, 32
   Bradshaw's [2].32; [3].*17*, 31, 32; [7].31
   Cannon [3].29, 30, 31
   Cheek's [11].13
   Complin's [3].31-2; [9].40; [11].36
   farms' [9].28
   Hatfield [3].6-7, 15, 29, 30, 31, 32, *32*; [7].28; [9].30; [11].9, 11, 36, *47*; 62, 85; [12].12
   New Town [11].43
   Searanke's [11].9, 11, 36, 58
   Sherriff's [3].8-9
   Whittingstall's [11].59
brewers [11].10, [11].87
Brewery Hill [3].7, *8*, *32*; [12].12
Brewery Yard [12].5
Brewhouse [9].*25*, 32, 44
Brewhouse cottage [10].*16*, 17
   OS grid ref. [10].31
   plan [10].*14*
   stair [10].15
Brewhouse Farm [9].47; [11].9
brewhouses [3].6, *8*, 11, 14
brewing [3].5, 6; [4].23
Briant, John [11].67-8
Briant, Mr. ("of Hartford") [7].8
Briars Lane [1].11; [2].*6*, *7*, *20*; [5].8, 16; [8].32
Briars Wood [2].4
Brice, William [4].16, 19
Brick Bat Field (Batsfield) [2].*20*, 21
Brick Field [1].*14*
Brick Ground [9].*24*
brick kiln [9].18
brick stacks [10].12-13
brickfields [11].63, 64
Brickhill Close [11].63

Brick-kiln Wood [10].7
   OS grid ref. [10].31
bricklayers [11].*12*, 34, 43, 44, **63-4**, 65, 86
brickmakers [11].16, 36, **63-6**, 86
brickmaking [1].19; [5].13; [10].7; [12].9
bricks [10].28
   price [10].25
Brickwall Hill [1].11; [5].9; [9].48; [11].61
Brickwood [1].16
brickwork, Old Palace [7].7; [10].7
bride ales [3].4
Bridewells
   Hatfield [6].8
   Hertford [6].17
   London [6].8
Bridge Piece field strip [2].19
Bridge Road [3].21; [10].14, 17, 31
bridges
   railway [5].13, 15, 16, 23
   Hunters [5].13
   responsibility for maintenance [6].12, 13
Briefs (Privy Council's letters) [6].16
Bright, Walter [4].22
Brightman, John [3].30
British and Foreign Schools' Society [8].10
British Museum [6].5
British Universal Directory [11].71
Brittain, Dr. Percy Morgan [11].83
Broad Oak Green [2].*20*, 23
Broad Oaks Junior School [8].15, 32
Broad Street [5].21
Broadwater [1].12
Broadwater Hundred [6].10
Broady, Joseph [7].22
Broady, Rev. William [7].22
Brocket family [2].12; [9].7, 41
   Brocket, Arthur Nall-Cain, 2nd Baron [7].16; [9].46

Brocket, John (of Roe Green) [2].15
Brocket, Sir John (J.P) [6].10; [11].55
Brocket, Mary [2].16
Brocket Hall [2].32; [11].54; [12].5, 26
   farm [9].6, 32
   sub-manor [10].9
   theft of lead [6].22
   in WWII [12].17
   OS grid ref. [10].31
Brocket Hall Corner [3].32
Brocket, Lady Elizabeth [1].*cover*
Brocket Manor [9].7
Brocket Park (Durantshide) [1].4, *6*, 6, *20*, 22-3; [2].13; [4].*26*; [11].58, 61
   farms [9].4, 18, 20, *24*
   pasture [9].31
Brook Field [2].17
Brook, Thomas [6].20
Brookbank, Joseph [4].13
Brookmans Park [5].16, 19; [7].29; [9].29
Brooks, Archibald (of Home Farm) [4].20, 22
Broom Field [2].*20*; [9].*24*
Broomfields [11].66
Brotherhood of Expiation [7].28
Brown, Gladys M.
   author *Parts* [2] *and* [9]
Brown, Henry (barber) [11].29
Brown, Monsignor Henry Barton [7].28
Brown, J. R. [2].3; [9].3
Brown (later Bassill), Mary [11].56
Brown, Nancy
   author *Part* [6]
Brown, V. W. [8].32
Broxbourne [4].11, 12, 13; [5].9, *10*
Bryan, Francis [4].11
Bryan, Isaac [11].63

Buckhamwykhyde (Bukhamwik, Bukhamwyk) *see* Woodside
Buckle, Christopher [4].19
Buckler, John: drawings by [1].10; [7].6; [8].10; [10].11; [11].75
Bugden [5].7
builders [8].9; [11].*12*, 34, 35, 36, 39, 41, 63-6, 84, 86
   family pedigrees [11].42
   table [11].34
building [6].12; [10].30
   costs [10].24-5
   materials [10].5, 25
Building Society [11].88
Bukhamwik (Woodside) *see* Bokenhamhide
Bull inn [3].13, *16*, 24, 29; [9].30; [11].59
Bull Stag Green [3].31
Bullens Green [2].22
Bullock Yard [9].33
Bull's Head [3].29
bungalows [9].43
Bunker, Ebenezer [11].71
Bunker, Henry [11].71
Bunneyfields House [1].10, 11; [10].6
Burch Wood [2].*28*
Burchell, Eliazer, school [8].*30*, 31
Burgess family [11].54
   Burgess, James [3].19; [11].39, 66
   Burgess, Thomas [4].19
   Burgess, William [11].66
burglary (larceny, theft) [6].7, 17, 18-19, 21-2
Burleigh School [8].32; [10].7
Burnestrete (Green Street) [1].21, 25
Burnham Close [2].19, *20*
Burr, Robert [2].15
Bury, Oliver [2].31; [11].40
Bury, Ursula [4].12

Burystead [1].17
buses [5].29-30, *31*
Bush Hall [2].*20*; [9].*24*, 44
Bush Hall school [8].*30*, 32
Busk, Jacob Han [4].14; [9].29
Busk, William [4].14
butchers [4].7; [9].34, 41; [10].19;
  [11].*12*, 14, 16, 24, 25,
  28-9, **31-3**, 40, 43, 84,
  85, 87
  Walby pedigree [11].30
Butchers Arms [3].*8*, 15, 23, 29
Butler, A. S. (of de Havilland)
  [12].26
Butler, Messrs. [11].14
Butler, Mr. (of Beech Farm) [2].13
Butterdale Pond [7].22
Butterfield family [11].54
buttery [10].15
Buxton, Misses [4].16
Buzza, Rev. W. A. [7].24
"By the Way" house [2].13
Byford, Daniel [4].23
Bymer Field [1].*13*
Byng, John [3].12, 27
By-Pass *see* Barnet By-Pass
Byron, George Gordon, 6th Baron
  [3].27
Byrt, Henry [6].20
Byrt, John [2].20

C

cabbage [9].47
Cachemaille Day, N. F. [7].20
Caesar, Misses: school [8].*30*, 32
Caesar (née Hall), Mrs. 84
cage [6].7-8
Cage Hill [3].*8*
Caledonian Railway [5].26
Caledonian Road [9].42
"California" *see* Newtown
Calverly (Caveller), Henry [11].64
Cambridge [5].26; [6].15
Cambridge Cattle Breeders'
  Association [9].44

Camfield Farm [5].8; [9].*25*
Camfield Place [1].*15*, 21; [12].6
Camp, J. [9].34
Camp, Mr. (of Roe Green Farm)
  [2].31
Camp, Mrs. (*fl.1889*) [7].26
camp, school [4].*4*, 5; [9].7
Camp, Thomas [7].26
Campfield Printing Works [5].19
Camvyle, William [1].22
candles [6].6; [11].17, 29
candlestickmaker [11].3
Canham family [11].54
  Canham, Catherine [8].27
  Canham, Joseph [3].24, *25*;
    [11].66
  Canham, Robert [3].24
  Canham, Sophia [11].26, 30
Cannon Brewery [3].29, 30, 31
Cannon, Mr. (farmer) [9].29
Carbone Hill [4].*4*, 5
Carlile family [4].26
  Carlile, Sir Hildred [4].14-16, 24,
    25
  Carlile, James W. [4].14
  Carlile, Mary [4].14
  Carlile, Prebendary [4].15
Carmel, Rev. Mother Mary [7].29;
  [8].32
Carmelite Nuns [7].28-9
Carnbrook, Agnes [11].55, 56
Carpenter, Agnes [11].13
Carpenter, Edmond [11].13
Carpenter, Thomas [6].16
carpenters [10].5, 6; [11].26, 35, 43,
  84, 86
carriers [11].25, 88
Carrington, John [3].6, 14, 19, 27
cars [5].29; [6].25; [7].13; [11].72,
  74
Carter, Francis [11].*12*
Carter, Mr. [6].13
Carter, Miss E. [8].12
Carter, Mrs. E. R. [3].26
Catemoye, P. C. [4].24

12

Cater, A. **[5]**.19
Cater, D. G. **[8]**.32
Cater, Jno. **[5]**.19
Cater, Jno. Jas. **[5]**.19
caterer **[11]**.26, 42
Catlin, William **[6]**.12
Catmoye (constable) **[6]**.20
cattle
   breeds **[9]**.20, 41, 43-4
   Cambridge Cattle Breeders'
      Association **[9]**.44
   markets **[9]**.33
   prices **[11]**.29
   transport **[5]**.8
cattle dealers **[11]**.86
Causton, Mr. (printer) **[11]**.15
Cave, Lady Otway **[9]**.29
Caveller family **[11]**.7, 16
   Caveller, Hugh **[11]**.16
Cavendish, Sir William **[4]**.11
Cavendish Arms **[3]**.*16*, 21, 22, 29
Cavendish Hall **[7]**.18, *27*, 31
Cavendish Way **[2]**.4, *6*, 32; **[5]**.23
Cecil Estate **[9]**.9, 29
Cecil Mill (Withy Mill) **[11]**.61
Cecil family [1].12, 16; **[2]**.13, 16;
      [7].27; **[11]**.7, 82
   and farmers **[9]**.45
   as Rectors **[7]**.**12-15**
   see also Cecill; Gascoyne-Cecil;
      Salisbury
Cecil, Rev. Charles
   as Rector **[7]**.12
Cecil, Lord Edward
   and Boer War **[12]**.7
Cecil, Lady Gwendolen **[2]**.31;
      [11].38
Cecil, William (*1714-40*)
   and school **[8]**.5
Cecil Crescent **[1]**.7; **[9]**.45; **[10]**.29
   OS grid ref. **[10]**.3
Cecil Saw Mill **[1]**.24, 25
Cecill, Henry **[6]**.16
Cecill, Phillip **[6]**.16

Cecill (Cecil), Robert (*fl.1652*)
      [6].16; **[7]**.11
Celtic missionary bishops **[7]**.5
cement **[10]**.8
   price **[10]**.25
Census **[11]**.54
   1801 **[5]**.4
   1841 **[2]**.14
   1851 **[2]**.25, **29-31**; **[5]**.13;
      [7].23, 30; **[9]**.31;
      [11].55, 65, 77
centenarian **[11]**.35
chalk **[7]**.7
   drawing **[2]**.21-2
   for marling **[2]**.21; **[9]**.14
   sub-soil **[1]**.*26*, 27; **[9]**.19
Chalk Dell **[2]**.21
Chalkdrawers Arms inn **[2]**.21
chalking **[9]**.37, 46
Chalkley, Mary **[11]**.30
Chamber of Trade **[11]**.46
Chamberlain, Neville **[12]**.*4*
Chambers, Sir Theodore **[12]**.*4*
chandlers **[11]**.15, 29, 87
Chantry Farm **[11]**.8, 27
Chantry Green **[2]**.27
Chantry Green House **[2]**.31
Chantry Lane **[2]**.*6*, *7*, 8, 13, 14, 16,
      20, 27, *28*, 31
   Spinney **[2]**.21
Chantry schools **[8]**.4
Chapel Treat **[8]**.18
chapels **[7]**.16, 23-7, *23*, 30, 31
   see also names
Chapman family **[11]**.36, 65-6, *65*
Chapman (builder) **[8]**.9
Chapman, Charles James **[11]**.34
Chapman, Dorcas **[11]**.30
Chapman, Eliza Marian **[11]**.34
Chapman, James (*b.1763*) **[11]**.*12*,
      34
Chapman, James (*b.1782*) **[11]**.34
Chapman, James (*b.1818*) **[11]**.34,
      43

Chapman, James (*d.1816*) **[11]**.65
Chapman, John (*b.1796*) **[11]**.27, 34
Chapman, John (*b.1818*) **[11]**.34, 43
Chapman, Lucy **[11]**.34
Chapman (publican?) **[3]**.32
Chapman, Sarah: school **[8]**.*30*, 31
Chapman, Sarah Elizabeth **[11]**.34
Chapman, Sophia **[11]**.34
Chapman, Thomas **[11]**.34
Chapman, W. **[12]**.25, 26
Chapman, W. A. J. **[8]**.32
Chapman, William **[11]**.34
Chapman's Field **[11]**.66
Chapman's Terrace **[11]**.36
Charity Commissioners **[7]**.14
Charity Land **[9]**.29
Charles I, King **[8]**.7
Charles II, King **[7]**.11
Charrington & Co. **[3]**.30, 31
Chatham line **[5]**.21
Chaucer, Geoffrey **[3]**.26
Chauncy, Sir Henry **[7]**.8
   History of Hertfordshire **[5]**.6
Chauntry Green **[2]**.23, 30; **[9]**.9
Chauntry Green Farm **[2]**.5, 7, *13*, 17, *20*
   1851 **[2]**.30
Cheek, John **[3]**.23
Cheek, Nathaniel **[3]**.23, 30, 32; **[5]**.9; **[11]**.13
Cheeseman, Rev. T. **[7]**.24
Chelsea Pensioner **[2]**.30
Cheltenham **[5]**.13
chemicals **[9]**.48
chemists **[11]**.23-4, 87
Chennels **[2]**.32
Chennels, Amelia **[2]**.32
Chequers Inn, Cromer Hyde **[3]**.*16*, 20-1, *20*, 29; **[11]**.58, 7
Chequers Inn, Fore Street **[3]**.6, *8*, 14, 29; **[11]**.6, 9, *12*
Chequers, The, Park Street **[10]**.17

Cherry Tree pub **[3]**.*16*, 21, 29
Chesher, George **[11]**.34, 43
Cheshunt **[4]**.5, 12, 13, 21, 24; **[9]**.9
Chessum family **[11]**.64
   Chessum, Andrew **[11]**.64
   Chessum, Elizabeth **[11]**.64
Chevall family **[4]**.16-17
   Chevall, Robert **[4]**.16
Cheyne, Elizabeth **[4]**.17
Child & Co., bank **[11]**.75, 76
children
   child labour **[8]**.20; **[9]**.26
   child mortality **[8]**.19
   of Roe Green, *1851* **[2]**.29-30
   in Union Workhouse **[8]**.23-4
   vagrants **[6]**.15
   see also schools
chimney sweep **[11]**.88
chimneys **[10]**.11, 12-13, 17, 19-20, 22
China **[7]**.14
china and glass dealers **[11]**.26, 34, 87
Chipperfield, John **[11]**.56
Chiswell Green **[7]**.18-19, *19*, *27*, 31
cholera **[5]**.13
Christ Church, Hatfield **[7]**.*27*, 30, 31
Christ Church, WGC **[7]**.*20*, 25, 32
Christ Scientist **[7]**.31
Christie's Brewery **[3]**.29, 30, 31
Christs Hospital **[4]**.22
Church family **[9]**.26, 31; **[11]**.74-6
   Church, Alice **[11]**.74
   Church, Sir Geoffrey **[6]**.28; **[11]**.76
   Church, John (*b.1724*) **[11]**.74-6
      coat of arms **[11]**.*75*
   Church, John (*c.1850*) **[8]**.11
   Church, John (farmer) **[9]**.26, 29
   Church, John (publican) **[3]**.30
   Church, Mary **[11]**.75
   Church, Mr. (landowner) **[6]**.19
   Church, Thomas **[11]**.74, 76

Church, William **[11]**.76
Church, Sir William Selby **[11]**.76
Church Cottage **[8]**.31; **[10]**.27;
   [11].67, 84
   OS grid ref. **[10]**.31
Church houses **[3]**.4
Church of the Blessed Sacrament
   and St. Theresa **[7]**.29,
   31
Church of England **[4]**.24; **[7]**.**5-9**,
   21; **[8]**.5; **[12]**.5
   Schools **[8]**.13, 15, 21, 31, 32
   Boys' School **[8]**.14, *30*, 31
   Girls' School **[8]**.9, 13-14
   Infants' School **[8]**.9
Church of St Francis **[7]**.*20*
Church Road **[12]**.15
Church (Back) Street **[1]**.24; **[3]**.*8*;
   [6].8; **[8]**.26; **[11]**.7, 9,
   12, 40, 44, 74, 80
   chapel **[7]**.26
   market **[11]**.5
   pubs **[3]**.15, 19, 29, 30, 31, 32;
   [5].9; **[11]**.15
   school **[8]**.8, 31
churches [7].5-31, *27*
   Anglican **[7]**.**15-21**
   see also Church of England
   attendance **[5]**.13; **[7]**.30
   clergy **[11]**.78-9, 86
   Methodist **[7]**.**25-7**
   in Newgate Street **[4]**.20, 23-4
   Non-conformist **[7]**.**21-5**
   Roman Catholic **[7]**.**27-30**
   Welwyn Garden City **[7]**.17, 19,
   20, 31
   Wesleyan **[7]**.**25-7**
   see also names of churches
churchwardens **[7]**.4, 7; **[8]**.11;
   [11].22, 28, 36, 61, 62
churchyard **[6]**.8; **[8]**.31; **[11]**.4, 31
Chyvall, Edmund **[4]**.16
C.I.D. **[6]**.27
circuses **[8]**.18
City of London **[11]**.54-5, 70, 75

Civic Central Fund **[12]**.15
civil actions **[6]**.19
Civil Resettlement Unit **[12]**.17
Civil War **[4]**.12; **[6]**.20
Clark family **[3]**.24
   Clark, Walter **[3]**.26
   Clark, William **[11]**.*12*
Clarke, Mary **[4]**.13
Clarke, Seymour **[5]**.18, 28; **[11]**.40
Clarke, William **[7]**.22, 26
clay **[1]**.19, 27; **[4]**.21; **[5]**.12; **[9]**.5;
   [10].6, 7; **[12]**.9
Clay, Geoffrey **[7]**.22
clergy **[11]**.78-9, 86
Clock House *see* Stonehouse
Clock pub **[5]**.30
clockmakers **[11]**.66, 86
clocks **[11]**.**66-7**
Clopton, William **[4]**.18
Close, The, Fore Street **[10]**.27
   OS grid ref. **[10]**.32
Clothall **[11]**.67
clothing **[9]**.10
clothing trades **[11]**.87
Cloughe, Robert **[8]**.4
clover **[9]**.17, 18, 19, 20, 21, 27, 47
clubs **[12]**.6
Coach and Horses **[3]**.*cover*, *17*, 29;
   [4].*4*, 6, 22, 23
coachbuilder **[11]**.86
coaches **[5]**.7, 8-9, 18
coaching **[3]**.9, 15
coachman **[11]**.88
Coade stone **[10]**.7
coal **[3]**.9; **[5]**.11, 19; **[11]**.62
coal dealers / merchants **[4]**.23;
   [11].42, 46, 87
coal-mines **[8]**.20
Cobb, Charles **[6]**.15
Cobb, James **[8]**.21
Cock alehouse **[3]**.*8*, 19, 29
cock fighting **[7]**.15
Cockaigne Housing Group **[12]**.11
Cocke family chart **[4]**.*12*
Cocke, Frances **[4]**.12

Cocke, Henry [4].11-12
Cocke, John [4].12
Cocke, Sir John [4].11, 12
Cocke, Ursula [4].12
Cockhouse [11].24, 25
Codicote [5].*11*
Cold Harbour (Coldharbour) farm [1].*15*; [4].*4*, 6, 21-2; [9].*9*, *25*, 34, 46, 47
Cole (Coles, Collem) family [1].22; [2].11-12, 24
Cole, Richard [2].11
Cole, William [2].11
Cole Green [2].22; [5].16, 23
Coleman Green [1].*25*; [2].22; [4].4; [9].*24*
Coleman, Jane Amelia [11].30
Coles, William [2].24
Colin atte Hide [1].21
Collarbone family [11].54
   Collarbone, George [11].40
   Collarbone, Joseph [11].40
collar-makers [11].*12*, 18-19; [11].86
College of Technology *see* Technical College
Collem family *see* Cole
Colliburn, Thomas [9].15
Collins, David [6].19
Collins, George [11].63
Collins, William [6].19; [9].15
Collinson, J. [4].3
Colne, river [1].25, 27; [12].25
Colney [4].19
Colney Hatch [5].19
Colney Heath [3].28; [9].35
Colonel's House *see* Batterdale House
Coly, William [6].21
Combination Act [6].17
Comet aircraft [5].4; [12].17, 18
Comet inn / Hotel [1].4, 5; [3].*cover*, 14-15, *16*, 29, 30; [5].18, *32*

Comet roundabout [1].4; [5].23, 30
Commissioners for Hertfordshire [3].4
Common Fields [1].18; [2].12, 15, 17-19, 32; [9].8-9, *24-5*, 29, 31
   Map (1829) [2].*18*
Common Market [9].48
common rights [1].15-16; [4].19; [6].6
Common Road [1].*14*
Commons, The [9].7
Commons Wood [9].33
Commonwealth [4].19; [8].7; [11].5
commuters [5].19
Company of Barber-Surgeons [11].79
Compasses alehouse / pub [3].*8*, 19, 29; [5].13; [11].25, 39
Complin, Francis Denyer [3].9; 11
Complin's Brewery [3].31-2; [9].40; [11].36
Comyn, John [4].9
concrete [10].8, 30
   wall [10].8
   OS grid ref. [10].31
Conduit Grove [1].*13*
Conduit Wood [10].7
   OS grid ref. [10].31
confectioner [11].87
Confirmation Service [3].19
Congregational Church [7].*20*, 24, 31
Conningsby, Henry [2].14
conspiracy [6].17
Constables [6].20-1; [11].42
   deputies [6].20-1
Contagious Diseases Act [9].34
contours [1].*26*, 27; [12].41
contractor [11].88
Convents [7].29
conveyors of vagrants [6].15
Cook, George [4].24
Coombe Wood [1].*8*, *9*

Co-op [12].12
Co-operative Society, St. Albans [12].11
Cooper, Gilbert [1].22
Cooper Horn, William [11].60
coopers [11].86
Cooper's Green [2].22; [7].18
   Forge Cottage [10].15, *16*, 17
   OS grid ref. [10].31
   plan [10].*14*
copyhold [6].9
cordwainers [11].*12*, 27, 86
corn [6].13; [9].34, 39
   export [9].17
   imports [9].26
   market [9].33
Corn Laws [5].12
corn merchants [11].86
Cornish, W. A. [12].5
Coroners [6].15; [11].79, 83
Corrall, Christopher [11].54-5, 70
Corrall, Edward [11].55
Corrall, John [6].17; [11].55
Corrall, Richard [11].54
corset maker [11].87
   Barclay Corsets [12].15
Cottage Hospital [12].15
cottages [10]. 21-5
   and *1588* Act [2].14
   Beaconsfield Road [10].24
   cost and plans [10].*14*, 24-5
   Flint, St. Albans Road [10].7, *8*, 28; [11].66
   OS grid ref. [10].31
   Park Street, sale [11].41, 43
   Police [8].15
   for railway workers [12].5
   Roe Green [2].25, 27, 30, 31
   Woodhall [10].12-13, *13*
Council houses [1].7; [10].29
Council Office [10].28
Countess Anne County School [8].32

Countess Anne's School [2].30; [7].8; [8].*cover*, **5-9**, *8*, 15, *30*, 31, 32
   Indenture [8].5
   Log Books [8].16-26
   Orders / sampler [8].6-7, *6*
   register, *1870* [8].*16-17*
   uniform [8].*2*, 5
Country Club [12].16
County Camp [4].*4*, 5; [9].7
County Council *see* Hertfordshire County Council
County Histories [4].3
County Library [12].22
County Police Act *1839* [6].22
County Police Force (Hertfordshire Constabulary) [6].22-8, *23, 25*
   Divisions [6].27
   Headquarters [6].*cover*
County Record Office [4].3; [6].21; [9].10, 26, 31; [11].3, 4, 20
Court Baron [6].5; [11].5
Court house [11].5
Court Leet [5].13; [6].5, 20; [11].5
Court Rolls [1].23; [2].12; [3].5; [6].*4*, 5, 6, 7, 20; [11].55
Courtenay, Gertrude [4].17
Courtenay, Henry, Marquis of Exeter [4].17
cowkeepers [11].86
Cowper, Dowager Countess [7].16
Cowper Estate [9].7
Cowper, George, 6th Earl
   inns owned by [3].30, 31
   and churches [7].16
   land owned by [9].29, 41
Cowper, Francis, 7th Earl [11].60
   and church [7].16
   school erected by [8].31
Cowpers Green [2].22
cows [11].29

cowsheds [9].39
Cox family [9].41; [11].7, 15, 16,
    24, 59, 60
Cox, Ann [11].59, 60
Cox, Emily [11].24
Cox, F. V. [8].32
Cox, J. (of Fore Street) [7].16
Cox, James [11].23-4
Cox, Jimmy [11].24
Cox, Mary Ann [11].16
Cox, (née Tharp), Mrs. [9].30
Cox (publican) [3].32
Cox, Sarah [9].41; [11].60
Cox, Stephen (c.*1848*) [7].16;
    [8].*30*, 31; [11].23, 24
Cox, Thomas (b.*1735*) [9].14-16
Cox, Thomas (d.*1787*) [11].16
Cox, Thomas (d.*1874*) [11].16
Cox, William [11].16, 59, 60
Crabb (publican) [3].31
Craft Guilds [8].4
craftsmen [11].86-7
    see also types of crafts
Cranborne School [8].32
Crawford family [9].38-40, 46
    Crawford, D. (farmer) [9].3, 41,
        45
    Crawford, Daniel (d.*1938*) [9].38-9
    Crawford, Daniel jnr. [9].40
Crawly, Robbert [9].15
Creamer Hide [7].21
Cresta Silks [12].15
Creswick, Thomas [6].17; [11].70
cricket [4].24
crime [6].7-9, 13, 28
    cases [6].16-19
    19c. 21-2
    see also types of crime
Cripps, Mary [11].56
Cripps, Thomas [6].12; [11].57
Cromer Hyde (Cromerhude,
    Cromerhyde) [1].*20*;
    [4].16, 26; [12].5, 26

farms [9].6, *24*, 29, 30, 32, 41,
    44, 46, 48
pubs [3].20-1, 29, 31
trades [11].54, 55, 56, 57, 58
Crook (Crok), Adam [1].22; [6].19
Crooked Billet pub [3].*16*, 26, *26*,
    30
crops [9].17
    protection [6].6-7
    rotation [9].20-1, 23, 27, 36, 39,
        40, 47
    see also types
Cross, Mrs. (of Rose and Crown)
    [4].23
Crosskesse house [11].25
Crow, Rev. T. [7].24
Crown Inn [3].*17*, 30; [4].5, 22, 23
Cubis, William [11].27
Cubitt, Joseph [5].12
Cuffley [4].24, 25
    Brook [4].*4*, 7
    Camp [4].*4*, 5; [9].7
    farms [9].7
    railway [5].*10*, *17*, 23, 26
    roads [5].7
Cull, E. F. [8].12
Cull, V. J. [12].7
Cumberland, Sarah [11].34
Cumberland, Sarah Susanna [11].34
Cumberland, Sophia [11].35
Cumberland, William [11].34, 35
Cupre, Simon [1].22
Curates *see* Faithfull, Rev. Francis
    Joseph; Hardcastle, Rev.
    W.E.; Hunt, Rev. J.B.;
    Karron, Rev. James;
    Marsham, Rev. Thomas;
    Peile, Rev. Benjamin;
    Robinson, Rev. Charles
    James
Currall, Richard [11].24
Currell family [11].43, 54-5, 58
    Currell, Lawrence [3].13
    Currell, Nicholas [11].57
    Currell, Richard [11].54, 57

Cussans, John Edwin
  History of Hertfordshire **[7]**.13;
  [8].22
Cutler, Sarah **[11]**.34
Cutler, Susanna **[11]**.34
cycle agent **[11]**.88
cycle shop **[11]**.74
cycling **[5]**.29

D

Dacre, Lord **[5]**.11
Dagmar House **[8]**.*30*, 31, 32
dairy farming **[9]**.34, 39, 42-3, 44, 46, 47
dairymen **[11]**.86
dame schools **[8]**.10
Danish invasion **[7]**.5
Dann, Nurse **[2]**.31
Daper, John **[3]**.5
Darby, John **[11]**.*12*, 13, 25, 83
Dare, John (schoolmaster) **[8]**.20, *30*, 31, 32
Dare, Mary Ann **[8]**.32
Darlington railway **[5]**.9
Darlington, William **[11]**.76
Darnicle Hill **[4]**.24
Dary, Thomas **[2]**.20
Dauber, Simon **[10]**.5
Daubere, Christian **[10]**.5
Davies, John **[6]**.17
Davies, Miss (schoolmistress) **[8]**.9
Davis, Mr. (farmer) **[9]**.34
Dawgs, William **[4]**.19
Dawnay Engineering **[12]**.15
Day, W. **[2]**.32
Days Mead **[2]**.32
de Havilland Aircraft Company
  [2].12-13, 14; **[12]**.16-17, 18, 20, 26
  aerodrome **[1]**.*5, 6*; **[2]**.4, 12-13, 24; **[5]**.4; **[9]**.35, 42, 43, 45-6; **[12]**.17, 18
  airfield **[1]**.27; **[5]**.30
  and Comet inn **[3]**.15

factory **[1]**.4, 6; **[4]**.25; **[12]**.*cover*
  pig farm **[9]**.48
  and railway **[5]**.23
  Telephone Exchange, sub-soil **[1]**.26
  Training School **[1]**.22
de Havilland, Maj. Charles **[11]**.85
de Havilland, Rev. Charles **[11]**.85
de Havilland, Sir Geoffrey **[11]**.85; **[12]**.16, 17
de Havilland, Martin **[11]**.85
de Havilland, Sir Peter **[11]**.85
de Soissons, Louis **[10]**.29; **[12]**.21-2, 25
De Voil, John **[11]**.35
Deacon, Alice **[11]**.74
Deacon, Daniel **[11]**.74
Deadmans Small Gains field **[4]**.21
Dearman, Abraham **[11]**.44
Dearman, Hannah **[11]**.44
debts **[9]**.13; **[11]**.21, 29, 32, 37
Ded Lane **[6]**.6
Dedemanne's Strat **[2]**.14
deer **[1]**.15
Deer, Isaac **[11]**.76
Deere, Thomas **[6]**.21
Deermar, Mr. (farmer) **[9]**.21
Defence of the Realm Act *1917* **[3]**.5
Defoe, Daniel **[5]**.7
Dell (innkeeper) **[3]**.23
Dell Croft **[2]**.16
Dell Mead **[2]**.21
Delle family **[2]**.24
  Delle, Robert atte **[2]**.24
  Delle, William de **[2]**.24
Dellfield **[2]**.13, 21
Dellfield Road **[1]**.7; **[11]**.66
dells **[2]**.**21-2**
demesne land **[1]**.17
Denny, Sir Anthony **[1]**.18
Denny, Sir Edward **[4]**.11
Denny, John **[6]**.6

deodand [11].6
depression [9].34, 43, 44, 46
Desborough, William Grenfell, 1st Baron [12].8
Development Corporations [2].16; [3].30; [11].3; [12].24
  first Chairman [12].9
  membership [12].25-6
  and new towns [12].20-2
  and railways [5].30
  and storm damage [12].24-5
Devil's Dyke, Wheathampstead [1].26
Dickens, Charles [3].27
  "Mrs. Lirriper's Lodgings" [3].27
  Oliver Twist [3].27; [11].77
Dickinson, Emma [8].9
Dickinson, Thomas [6].18
diet
  19c. [7].14
  20c. [12].14
Digswell (Diggwall) [4].19; [9].16; [11].59
Digswell Arts Trust [12].24
Digswell Lake Society [12].24
Dill, John [6].17
Dimsdale, Charles [4].20
Dinn (*fl.1826*) [6].18
Dinsley, Robert [11].6
Diocesan Bishop [11].79
Diocesan Board [8].11
Dioceses [7].5
Dip Dell [2].21
Directories [11].86, 87, 88
disease [9].34
displaced persons camp [4].25
dissenters [7].21-5
ditches [6].6
doctors [11].76, 78-85, 87
Dogenhyde (Doggenhyde) [1].10; [9].6
Dognell Green [11].55, 71
Dolamores Pot Bar [5].8
Dollimore, A. A., shop [11].6

Dollimore's shop [3].10
Domesday [10].10
Domesday Book [1].22, *22*, 23; [5].4; [7].6, 9; [9].6
Dominican Sisters [7].30
Doncaster [5].*11*, 25, *29*
Dorchester Diocese [7].5
Douro Arms [3].30
Down (Down's, Downe's, Downs) Farm [1].18, 22; [2].5, 6, 7, **8-11**, *20*, 24, *28*; [9].10, 35, 46; [11].60
Downe, Johanna [6].7
Downe, John [2].5, 9
Downs [6].9; [9].*24*
Drage, Charles (*c.1872*) [8].26
Drage, Dr. Charles [11].82-3, *82*
Drage, Elinor Margaret [11].82
Drage, Dr. Lovell [11].83
Drage, Mrs. [8].23
Drage, R. L. [11].23
drainage [9].14, 20, 21-2, 23, 37, 39, 46
drapers [6].13; [11].10, *12*, 13, 15, 22, 26, 27, 28, *28*, 77, 87
Dray Horse tavern [3].*8*, 15, *18*, 30; [11].71, 74; [12].5
dress makers [11].87
drill instructor [11].88
Drive, The [9].41
drove roads [5].8
druggists [11].87
drums [11].21
Drury Bros. [3].7
Duane, W. M. [8].32
Duchy of Lancaster [4].10
Duck Lane *see* Park Street
Dudley, Jacob [11].34
Duffyll, Edward [11].79
Dulsome Green [2].*28* (*1851*) [2].30
Dunham family [11].54, 77-8
Dunham, Ann Sophia [11].26
Dunham, Benjamin [11].43, 66

Dunham, Charles [8].20
Dunham, Francis [11].15
Dunham, James Benjamin
    [11].77-8
Dunn family [11].9
  property owned by [11].8
Dunn, Francis [11].10, 13
Dunn, James [11].9, 10, 13, 25
Dunn, John [11].10, 13, 25
Durantshide *see* Brocket Park
Durham [5].*11*

E

East Field [2].*18*, 19
East Indian Chief alehouse [3].8, 19,
    26, 30; [8].10; [10].27;
    [11].6, 24
  OS grid ref. [10].31
Easton, G. D. [11].35
Eaton, William [2].27
Ede, J. Chuter [6].25
Edgar, King [1].16, 24; [7].6
Edinburgh, Duke of [5].4; [12].26
education [2].30; [8].4, 20
  see also schools
Education Acts [8].8, 20, 26
Edward I, King [7].7
Edward II, King [6].10
Edward III, King [4].9, 10; [6].10
Edward VI, King [1].16, 17; [8].16
Edward VII, King [7].13; [8].18;
    [12].5, 6
  in Hatfield [12].5
Edwardes, William [11].53
Edwards, Thomas [11].34
Edwards, William [7].22
Eight Bells pub [1].4; [3].*cover*, 8,
    15, 18-19, 28, 30; [5].9;
    [11].6, 8, *12*, 13, 62, 64
  Dickens writes of [3].27
  publicans [3].23; [11].13, 62, 64
  riot in [3].18; [5].12
  spoon stolen [3].23; [6].17
Elizabeth I, Queen [1].16; [4].12;
    [6].8; [8].16

childhood [1].12; [2].10
  as Princess [1].16; [4].11;
    [11].59
  reign [2].10
  and Tolmers [4].18
Elizabeth II, Queen [12].15
Elizabeth de Jersey [11].85
Ellen brook (Ellenbrook) [1].*6*, 6;
    [2].17, *28*; [5].30;
    [7].29; [11].58
  housing estate [2].4, 19
Ellenbrook Lane [2].*18*
Elliott family [11].54
Elliott, Ellis [11].63
Elliott, Mary [11].80
Ellis, Phil. [7].22
Ellis, Thomas (Dissenter, *fl.1701*)
    [7].21
Ellis, Thomas (*fl.1749*) [11].19
Ellis, Wynn [4].14, 23, 25
Elm Gardens [12].15
Ely [1].22, 24; [7].5; [10].5
  Abbey [1].24; [7].5, 6
  Abbots [1].16, 23; [7].5
  Bishopric [7].5, 7
  Bishops *see* Bishops of Ely
employment [4].25; [12].14-15, 17,
    20
enclosure [6].11
  Great Wood [1].16; [4].19, 21,
    22
Enclosure Acts [9].9
Endersbie, Richard [11].67
Endymion Road [8].13, *14*; [10].28
  OS grid ref. [10].31
Enfield [5].23, 26
Enfield Chace Foxhounds [4].6
English, Abraham [6].24
Ensom, Thomas [3].21, 32
entail [4].13
Epsom [11].61
Ermine Street [1].25; [5].5
Essendon [1].*20*; [4].10, 13
  brewing [3].6; [11].9
  churches [7].15, 29

farms [9].6, 7; [11].61, 62
trades [11].9, 59, 74; [12].11
Essendonbury [9].37
Essex, Arthur Algernon Capell, 6th
    Earl of [9].34
Estate Duty [9].30
Etheldreda, St. [1].24; [7].6; [11].4
evacuees [8].25
Evangelical Revival [7].21
Evans, Rev. Daniel [8].31; [11].25
Evans, Louise C. [8].27
Eversall, Sarah [11].16
Ewer, Stephen [4].12-13, 14, 16
Ewington family [11].54
Exeter [7].13
Eya, Philip de [7].6

F

Factory Acts [8].20
Fair Days [8].16
Faircloth, John Palmer [11].36
Faircloth, Joseph [3].14
Faircloth, William [11].36
Fairfolds Farm [9].41
fairs [9].16; [11].4, 7, [11].73
Fairs, Tom [12].24
Faithfull, Caroline [8].*12*
Faithfull, Rev. Francis Joseph
    [5].11, 13; [6].21;
    [7].14, 26; [11].70
    J.P. [6].22
    and Parsonage [10].10-11
    schools [8].4, 11, 30, 31
fallowing [9].21, 23
Falls [4].22
families [11].3-11, 40-6, 51-85
    farming [11].60-2, 84-5
    migration into Hatfield [11].53-4
    of Roe Green [2].24-5
    tradesmen's [11].42
    see also names
famine fast, *1847* [5].13
Fanshawe, Katherine [4].12
Fanshawe, Sir Thomas [4].12

Fanshawe, Thomas jnr. [4].12
Farington [3].9
farm houses [10].12-21
Farm, The (Northcotts), [11].9
farmers [11].16, 34, 86
    combined occupations [9].34
    families [11].60-2
    from other English counties
        [9].31
    from Scotland
        in *19c.* [9].34-6, 43
        in *20c.* [9].44-5
farming, Golden Age of [9].35
farms [9].4-48
    16-17c. [9].9-12
    18c. [9].13-18
    later *18c.* [9].18-23
    19c. [9].23-42
    1824 [9].29-30
    20c. [9].42-8
    boundaries [2].7
    cattle *see separate entry*
    and enclosure [9].9
    fee farm rent [8].5, 7-8
    names [9].4-5
    Newgate Street [4].20, 21-2
    origins [9].6-9
    Roe Green [2].**5-17**, *18*
    size [9].**19, 28**
    stock animals [9].43-4
    see also arable land; *farm names*
Farr family [9].30, 31; [11].61
Farr, Ann [2].25
Farr, Frederick [7].16
Farr, George [11].61
Farr, Miss (schoolmistress) [8].16, 26
Farr, William [6].17
Farraway, John [11].76
Faulkner, Geoffrey [3].30
Faye's shop [3].14
Fearnley family [9].41
Fearnley, Edmund [11].16, 59
Fearnley, Sarah [11].59
Fearnley (née Tharp), Mrs. [9].30

Fearnley-Whittingstall family
  [11].59-60
Feathered World, The [9].40
fee farm rent [8].5, 7-8
Feld, William [6].7
Felde, John [6].5
fellmongers [11].39, 40, 86
Fellowship House [7].*20*, 31
Ferrers, Elizabeth [4].9, 12
Ferrers, Sir John [4].12
Ferrers, Knighton [4].12
Festival of Britain [10].30
Fetcham, Surrey [4].19
Fever (Feather) Dell Common
  [2].15, 16, 19, *20*, 21, 32
Fiddle Bridge [9].36
Fiddle Dell Field (Fiddle Field)
  [2].19, *20*, 21
"Fiddle" public houses [2].19, 27
  New Fiddle [2].27
  Old Fiddle [2].27
  sign [2].*26*
Field (prisoner) [6].21
Field (railway employee) [11].40
Field, Joseph [3].7; [9].30
Field, William [6].4
fields [2].*20*; [9].*4, 5 8, 9*
  names [2].16, **19-21**; [9].7, 9, 27
  types [9].4-5
Film Studio [12].15
Finchley [11].33
Fine-Fare [12].12
Finsbury Park [5].19, 21
Fiott, Carteretta [11].85
fire
  compensation [6].15, 16
  at Hatfield House, *1835* [3].27;
    [11].82
  in railway tunnel [5].28
Fire Brigade [11].73
fireboot [1].16
fireplace [10].12, 13
First Church of Christ Scientist
  [7].*20*
fish [11].61

fish pond [1].*18*
fishing [6].16
fishmongers [11].*12*, 87
Fitz-Symon [1].21; [9].5
Flaunden Chapelry [1].5
Flemish settlers [3].6
Fletcher, William [2].20
Fleur de Lys [3].30
Flexmore, Simon [10].19
flint [2].22; [10].7
Flint Cottages, St. Albans Road
  [10].7, *8*, 28, [11].66
  OS grid ref. [10].31
Flitney family [11].54
Flitney, Clifford [12].17
Flitney, George [12].3, 5, 7, 17,
  26
Flitney, Ted [12].17
florist [11].88
Flower, Richard [3].30
flower show [8].17
Flowers Breweries [3].29
flying bombs [6].26, *26*; [8].15
Flying Scotsman [5].*cover*, 23
Folly Archway [2].9
food *see* diet *and types of food*
Foot and Mouth disease [9].34
Football Pool [7].29
Ford, Ann [11].56
Ford, Elizabeth [8].20
Ford, John [6].19
Fordham, John [3].30; [9].29, 30
Fore (Front, High) **Street** [1].4, 10,
  16, 24; [6].24; [7].16;
  [8].21, 22, 26; [11].*8,
  23*, 80
  church and Vicarage [7].6, 12
  extent [11].6
  houses [10].25, 27-8, *29*;
    [11].54
  inns [5].9
  market [11].5, 6
  North Side [11].8, **24-9**
  Nos. 15-17 [10].25
  Nos. 44 and 46 [10].25, 27

OS grid ref. **[10]**.31
pubs **[3]**.6, 14, 15, 19, 23, 27,
  29, 30, 31
Rectory **[10]**.15
  plan **[10]**.*14*
road surfacing **[5]**.8
Royal Visit **[12]**.*6*
schools **[8]**.5, 10, 11, 31, 32;
  [11].25
South Side **[11]**.11-24
shops and trades **[11]**.11-29, *17*,
  40, 61, 70, 76, 77, 78,
  80, 81, 83, 84, 85;
  [12].12
forest **[1]**.22, 23, 27; **[2]**.4, 10; **[4]**.6;
  [9].6-7, 9
  clearing **[1]**.23; **[4]**.6
  see also woodland
Forest, John **[1]**.22
Forestar, Robert **[4]**.7
Forester, Robert **[4]**.7
Forester, William **[1]**.22
foresters **[11]**.86
forge **[4]**.*4*, 22, *22*
Forge Cottage, Cooper's Green
  [10].15, *16*, 17
  OS grid ref. **[10]**.31
  plan **[10]**.*14*
Forrest, Sir Antonie **[4]**.21
Fortescue family **[4]**.8, 10, 16
  Fortescue, Henry **[4]**.11
  Fortescue, Sir John **[4]**.10-11
Foster, John **[6]**.19
Foundry **[12]**.15
Fountayne, Jane **[4]**.18-19
Four Horsehoes **[3]**.26
Fowler family **[9]**.40
Franceis, Symon **[1]**.22
Frank family **[9]**.31
Fray, Elizabeth **[4]**.17
Free Church **[7]**.*20*, 31
Free School **[8]**.*30*, 31
Freeman, John **[3]**.10, 30
Fremantle, Col. F. E. **[12]**.*4*
French Horn **[3]**.30

French Horn Lane [1].*18*; **[2]**.12;
  [5].6; **[7]**.11, 28
  chapel **[3]**.19; **[7]**.26-7
  families and trades **[11]**.36, 38,
    63, 71
  inns **[3]**.30
  Malting Mead houses **[2]**.31;
    [3].9
  maltings **[3]**.9
  Police **[6]**.23, 25
  Rectory *see separate entry*
  schools **[8]**.11, 17, 32
Freshwater, Francis **[11]**.27
Frewen, Sarah **[11]**.69
Frewen, Thomas **[11]**.69
Friday Field **[4]**.21
Front Street *see* Fore Street
Fulk atte Water **[1]**.22
Full Measure **[3]**.30; **[11]**.*cover*
Fuller, Alfred Otway **[11]**.26
Fuller, Dr. Thomas **[11]**.80
Fuller, Thomas **[4]**.18
fulling mills **[6]**.11; **[11]**.69
furnishers **[11]**.42
furniture **[9]**.10-11
furniture dealers **[11]**.87
Further Butty Piece field strip **[2]**.19
Furze Grove **[2]**.21
Fysshe, John **[6]**.6-7

G

Gacelin, Geoffrey **[4]**.8
Gacelyns manor **[4]**.7, 8-10, 18
Gainsborough, Thomas
  Duchess of Devonshire **[4]**.14
gale, *1957* **[12]**.24-5, *24*
Gallery of Antiques **[10]**.27
Galley Common **[2]**.*20*
Galley Corner **[2]**.14
Galley Corner Turnpike Trust **[5]**.7-
  8, 9
"Galley Croft" (house) **[2]**.14; **[3]**.9;
  [11].84
  school **[8]**.32
gamekeepers **[11]**.86

games [3].5
Gamkin, John [6].21
Gamon, Christopher [7].22
Gape Estates [2].12
Gape family [2].12, 13; [9].34;
    [10].22
Gape, Mr. (farmer) [9].29
garage
    Motor Works [11].72-3, 73;
       [12].7, 16
    petrol station [4].22
    space [11].72
    Waters' [1].10; [7].28
Garden Cities [12].8
Garden City Company [3].29;
    [12].9, 20
Garden House [10].28; [11].25
    OS grid ref. [10].31
Garden Village [1].6; [12].16
gardeners [11].86
Garland, John [8].8
Garlick, Rev. G. [7].24
Garston [9].44
Gascoyne Cecil School [8].32
Gascoyne-Cecil, Rev. Lord William
    as Rector [3].19; [7].12, 13-14,
       21; [8].18
    article by [7].14-15
Gate Piece field strip [2].19
Gatehouse (Salisbury Arms) [3].11,
    31; [8].10; [10].27-8
Gates, Mary [6].16
Gathard, Maria [11].42
Gaussen, Mrs. [9].29
Gaussens, Mr. (of Brookmans Park)
    [1].8
Gaylord, Eliza [8].23
Geary, Sir William [4].19
Gentleman's Magazine [11].35, 57
Geoffrey de Stoke [1].21
geology [1].*26*; [9].4, 19
George III, King [11].81
George V, King [7].13; [8].18
George VI, King [6].26; [8].26

George Fields [11].*8*
George, George [11].17
George inn [3].*8*, 10-11, 19, 28, 30,
    31, [11].60, 80
    rooms [3].10
Gerard, William [6].6
Gervase de Walkemede [1].22
Gibbs, Geoffrey [11].40
Gibbs, Archdeacon Kenneth [7].12;
    [10].11
Giddins, David [6].18-19
Gilbert, Ann [3].24
Gilbert, John [3].24
Gilbey's Shilling Moselle [11].23
Giles, L. G. [8].32
Gillians family [11].54
Gillon, Rebecca [8].28, 29
Girls Grammar School [8].32
Gisborne, Thomas
    Essays on Agriculture [9].2
glass: price [10].25
glass dealers [11].26, 34, 87
Glassbrook (Glazebrook), Henry
    (prisoner) [6].21
Glasscock, Thomas [11].64
glaziers [11].11, 14-15
Glebe [1].*14*, 17, 24; [7].9, 11;
    [11].*8*
Glebe Close [1].*18*
Glover, Robert [6].16
Glover and Co. brewery [3].7
glovers [11].26, 27, 40
Glyn, Mills and Company [4].20
Goddard, Rev. Paul [7].18
Godfrey, John [7].22
Golden Age of Farming [9].35
Golden Jubilee, *1887* [8].18
Golders Green [5].29
Goldings Farm [11].80
Goldings Police Station [6].*23*, 25
Goldsmiths' Company [11].55
golf course [4].16
Goodere, Audrey [4].18
Goodere, Francis [4].18-19

25

Goodere, Henry **[4]**.18, 19
Goodere, Sir Henry **[4]**.18, 19
Goodrich House **[10]**.27, 28, *29*;
  [11].25
  OS grid ref. **[10]**.31
Goodrick, Thomas, Bishop of Ely
  [1].18-19; **[7]**.7
Gosling, Reginald **[12]**.21, 25
Gosling Stadium **[12]**.9
Gosmore farmland **[9]**.30
Gosmore house **[3]**.32; **[10]**.19, 20
  OS grid ref. **[10]**.31
Gothic style **[10]**.28
Gracemead cottages **[12]**.5
grammar schools **[8]**.4, 32
Grantham **[5]**.25
Grass Belt **[9]**.46
Grave, Rev. William Cecil **[7]**.13
gravel **[1]**.27; **[5]**.12, 15, 23; **[9]**.19;
  [12].9
  pits **[6]**.12
  price **[10]**.25
  Ryder's Seed Trial Ground
    [2].14
  workings **[9]**.46
Gravel Field **[6]**.21
Gray family **[2]**.29-30, 31; **[11]**.54,
  71-2
  Gray, Daniel **[6]**.21; **[11]**.71
  Gray, Henry W. **[3]**.3; **[11]**.3
    co-author Part **[3]**; *author Part*
    [11]
  Gray, James (*b.1860*) **[11]**.71, *71*,
    72-3
  Gray, John **[11]**.72
  Gray, Richard **[11]**.72
  Gray, William **[2]**.13; **[11]**.72
Graye, William **[4]**.11
Gray's Motor Works **[11]**.72-3, *73*;
  [12].7, 16
Great Down **[2]**.*20*
Great Eastern Railway **[5]**.*10*, 16,
  26

Great North Road (A.1000;
  London Road) **[1]**.3, **8-
  11**, *5*, *8*, *9*, *13*, 16, 20;
  [5].**6-9**, *8*, 30, *32*; **[6]**.25;
  [9].45; **[12]**.8
  c.1603 **[1]**.*13*
  early *19c.* **[1]**.*9*, *10*
  after *1850* **[1]**.*8*
  cafés on **[12]**.15
  diversion for railway **[3]**.12;
    [5].12, 15; **[11]**.40
  Edward VII on **[12]**.5
  families and trades **[11]**.6, 9, 32,
    71, 74, 78
  in Hatfield Park **[1]**.*12*
  houses **[10]**.8, 28
  inns **[3]**.*8*, 9, 30. 31, 32; **[11]**.24
  maintenance **[4]**.24
  No. 69 **[10]**.7
  No. 73 **[10]**.28
  OS grid ref. **[10]**.31
  Roman? **[1]**.25
  schools **[8]**.12, 17, 25
Great Northern inn **[3]**.*8*, 30; **[5]**.13;
  [11].74
Great Northern Railway (G.N.R.)
  [2].31; **[5]**.5, *10*, *11*, 12-
  13, 15-16, 18, 19, 21;
  [7].14; **[11]**.40, 88
  employees, *1851* **[11]**.40
  employment **[5]**.14
  map **[5]**.*11*
  speed **[5]**.26-7
Great Northern Railway Company
  [1].8; **[3]**.20, 29;
  [10].29; **[12]**.5
Great Stables **[8]**.8-9
Great Thistley Field **[2]**.16
Great Western Railway (G.W.R.)
  [5].26
Great Wood **[1]**.15-16, *15*, 19, *20*;
  [2].8; **[10]**.5, 6, 7, 12;
  [11].63
  enclosure **[1]**.16; **[4]**.19, 21, 22

gate [1].22
land [1].27
Newgate Street [4].*4*, 6
Symonds Hyde [1].6
Tolmers [4].16, 22, 26
Greater London Plan [12].18
Greek [8].4
Greemore (Grimblecroft, Grumblecroft) field [2].16
Green Belt [4].25; [9].48; [12].8-9, 19-20
Green (Greene) family [2].12
　Green, J. W, [3].29
　Green, John [2].24; [3].12
　Green, Pardoe [6].17
Greenfoot (Green Foot) Cottages [2].*cover*, 25, 27
Green Lanes [1].11, *14*, 25; [5].8, 30; [8].32
Green Lanes School [1].6
Green Man inn *1850* [5].13
Green Man pub, Back (Church) Street [3].10, 30
Green Man pub, Fore Street [3].*8*, 15, 23, 30; [11].13
Green Man, Mill Green [3].10, *16*, 30; [11].71
Green Man, Potters Bar [1].11
Green Street (Burnestrete) [1].21, 25, *25*
Green Street Cottage [10].19
　OS grid ref. [10].31
　plan [10].*14*
Greenaway coach-house [3].30; [11].13, 79, 83
Greenfoot Cottages [2].27
Greenham family [11].54
　Greenham, Arthur [8].20
　Greenham, Charles [8].20
greens (settlements) [2].5, **22-3**
　village green [4].24
Greenstead [10].6
Gregory family [11].54
　Gregory, (Miss) E. [8].21-2

Gregory, John (carpenter) [11].26
Gregory, John (grocer) [11].26
Gregory, Margaret [11].26
Gregory, Thomas (*d.1879*) [11].26
Gregory, Thomas (*d.1910*) [11].26
Gregory de Stoke [2].8
Grenham, Thomas [9].15
Grey, Lady Jane [4].17
Grey, William [6].6
Greyhound inn [1].9; [3].12, *16*, 27, 28, 30; [9].*24*, 26, 30; [11].75, 76
Griffin inn [3].30
Grimes Brook [4].*4*, 5, 24
Grinley, Charles: *History of the Great Northern Railway* [5].28
grocers [11].*12*, 15-19, 26, 34, 44, 87
　family pedigrees [11].42
Groom family [11].54
　Groom, Frank [11].14
　Groom, James [11].14
　Groom, William [11].14
Ground Lane [9].43; [11].63, 64
　cottages [10].24
　OS grid ref. [10].31
groves [2].4
Grovestock family [11].42, 43, 54
　Grovestock, Richard [11].42
Grubb, Ann [11].15, 16
Grubb, Joshua [11].16
Grumble Croft [2].*20*
Gubbins (Gobions), North Mymms [2].9
Guessens Court [12].11
guest houses [3].4
Guild of Barbers [11].79
Guinness Trust [12].22
Gun pub [3].*17*, 18, 21, 24, *25*, 30; [5].13; [6].24; [10].28
　OS grid ref. [10].3
Gunton, Richard [7].14
Gurney, Baron [6].24
guttering [10].7

H

Hadley Wood [5].26
Hadlin, Thomas [11].71
Haggard, Sir (Henry) Rider [9].36-7, 42, 43
  Rural England [9].*35*
Hagger, Daniel [11].71
Haile, William [6].16
hairdressers [11].27
Hakes, Elizabeth [11].56
Haldens [12].24
Hale, Joseph [2].27
Hale, Michael [6].15
Halevy, Élie [4].3
Hall family [11].9, 84, 85
  Hall, Charles [7].17; [11].13
  Hall, Charles Vincent Ross [11].85
  Hall, Dr. (late *19c.*) [11].83, 84
  Hall, Dr. (of Hill House) [2].25
  Hall, Dr. Charles [11].84-5
  Hall, Elizabeth [11].30
  Hall, James [11].84
  Hall, M. W. [2].*18*
  Hall, Margaret [11].85
  Hall, Martha [3].31
  Hall, Mr. (farmer) [9].29
  Hall, William [2].25, 27; [11].*12*, 32, 84, 85
Hall Grove [7].20
Halsey family [3].24
Hamilton, Emilia [11].84
Handside (Hane's Hyde, Haneshyde, Hauntside) [1].*20*; [4].*26*
  Farms [9].6, 7, 10, 14, *24*, 29, 30, 31, 32, 42, 45
    Lower Handside Farm [9].41; [11].60
    Upper Handside Farm [11].59
  shops [12].12
  well [12].9
Handside Lane [9].41
  houses [12].9

Hankin family [11].54
  pedigree [11].26
Hankin, Ann Maria [11].26
Hankin, Arthur [3].15, 27; [11].82
Hankin, Arthur William [11].26, 27, 43
Hankin, Charles [11].26, 43
Hankin, Esther Sigrave [11].30, 85
Hankin, Ethel [11].26
Hankin, Frederick John [11].26, 27
Hankin, Henry [11].26, 27
  shop [11].27, *28*
Hankin, Henry Hudson [11].26, 27, 28
Hankin, James [6].19
Hankin, John (c.*1874*) [7].24
Hankin, John (of Baldock, b.*1785*) [11].26
Hankin, John (draper, b.*1820*) [11].26, 27
  shop [3].14; [11].27, *28*
Hankin, Joseph [11].26
Hankin, Mary Ann Sarah [11].10
Hankin, Oliver [11].26
Hankin, Rosa [11].26
Hankin, S. C. [5].29
Hankin, Sarah [11].26
Hankin, Sophia [11].26
Hankin, Stanley Coles [11].26, 27
Hankin, William (glover and tailor, d.*1851*) [11].26, 27, 28
Hankin, William (tailor, d.*1870*) [11].26
Hardcastle, Mr. (curate) [7].19-20
Harding, James [7].21
Harditch, James [6].17
Hardum, Charles [11].15
Hardum, Joseph [11].28
Hardum, Lancelot [11].*12*, 14-15, 19
Hardum, Thomas [11].14, 15

Hare family [3].9, 10, 31; [11].9, 36, 52
  property owned by [11].*8*
Hare, Edward (*d.1742*) [11].10, 33
Hare, Edward (*d.1747*) [11].10, 33
Hare, Mary (née Searancke) [11].36-7
Hare, Samuel (baker) [11].10, 33
Hare, Samuel (maltster) [3].10; [11].10, 33, 36-7, 66
Hare, Rev. Samuel [3].10, [11].10
Hare, Susannah [11].33
Hare Malting [3].*8*; [8].11
Harefield [5].6
Harker (railway employee) [11].40
Harman, Clemencia [6].6
Harman, Gerard [6].5, 6
Harpenden [1].6; [3].7; [11].58, 70
  railway [5].18
Harper family [11].25
Harpesfeld, John de [2].24
Harpesfield [1].20, 25
Harpesfield Hall Farm [12].16-17
Harpesfield Manor [4].*26*
Harpsfeld Hall [2].24
Harpsfield Farm [9].32, 45
Harpsfield Hall [2].12, 13, 24, *28*; [9].*24*, 35-7, *35*
Harras, James [3].23; [6].17
Harrington, Thomas [6].12
Harrison, Sarah [6].15
Harrow family [11].63-4
  Harrow, Andrew [11].64
  Harrow, John [3].9, 30; [11].38, 64
  Harrow, William (*c.1647*) [11].64
  Harrow, William (Fudge, *d.1763*) [3].28; [11].64
Hart family [2].25, 30; [11].24-5, 54
Hart, G. [4].3
Hart, Jane [2].25
Hart, John [11].25
Hart, Mr. (b.1872) [2].14

Hart, Mrs. (of Holly Cottage) [2].30
Hart, William [11].*12*, 24, 32
harvest [9].15, 17, 36
Harvey, Thomas [11].15
Haseldine Meadows [2].32
hat makers [2].30; [8].23; [11].87
hat trade [5].18, 19; [11].22
Hatfield
  changes [1].4-25
  mediaeval [1].20-1
  in *1850* [5].13-14
  c.1860 [5].*14*
  since *1960s* [1].1
  name [1].24
  old [1].4; [11].3
  see also Hatfield Parish; maps of Hatfield; New Town (Hatfield)
Hatfield and St. Albans Railway [5].15, 16, 18
Hatfield Brewery [3].6-7, 15, 29, 30, 31, 32, *32*; [9].30; [11].9, 11, 36, *47*; 62, 85; [12].12
Hatfield Bury [1].17; [9].9
Hatfield Home Park [1].24
Hatfield House [1].4, 5, 6, *8, 9*; [2].*28*
  archives [5].13; [6].*4*, 5; [7].14; [9].*8*; [11].5
  bell and clock [11].67
  building [1].12; [10].7, 8; [11].63
  and church [7].8
  entrance [1].4
  farms [9].18, 20, 22
  fire, *1835* [3].27; [11].82
  gates [7].9
  OS grid ref. [10].31
  and railway [5].9
  and schools [8].14-15, 17, 24
  storm damage [12].25
  in WWI [12].7
  in WWII [12].17

Hatfield Hyde (Hide) [1].*20*, 21, 22;
    [2].24; [4].*26*; [12].6, 22
  church [7].16, 20, 21
  farms [9].6, 7, 10, 32, 33, 45;
    [11].61, 72
  map [9].*8*
  pubs [3].21, 23, 25, 30, 31, 32
  school [8].*30*, 31
Hatfield Manor [1].16, 17, 19-20,
    23; [4].11, 16, 21
  descent [1].**16**, 18-19
  fairs [11].4
  farms [9].9
  order in [6].**5-9**
  papers [2].3
  see also Court Rolls; Lord of
    the Manor
Hatfield Park [1].6, *6*, *9*; [11].78
  in *1603* [1].12, *14*
  farms [9].7, *24*, 32, 33, 40, 44,
    47, 48
  pasture [9].31
  roads [1].11, *12*
  school in [8].5-6, 17
  Woodside Gate [1].9
  in WWI [12].7
Hatfield Park Lodge [2].31
Hatfield Parish [1].4, 6; [2].4; [4].5
  1927 [1].*6*
  boundaries [1].*6*, *15*; [2].*20*;
    [5].13, 16; [7].15; [9].4
  Hatfield South [7].29
  natural features [1].*26*, 26-7
  population [5].4
  records [7].4
  school for [8].5
Hatfield School [2].12; [8].32;
    [9].47
Hatfield Wood *see* Great Wood
hats
  Brazilian [2].30
  straw [2].30; [5].18, 19; [8].23
  top hats [6].22
Hauntside (Hane's Hide) [9].6
Hawker Siddeley Aviation [12].18

Hawkes, Susan [6].13
Hawkins, John [7].22
Hawkins, William [6].21; [11].25
hay [9].17, 19
Haydon, Daniel [11].75
Hayfield Thorpe [11].59
Hayman, Ailward [1].21
Hayman, William [1].21
Hazel Grove (Hazelgrove) [2].4, 7,
    10, 17, *20*, 21; [8].32;
    [10].8
  OS grid ref. [10].31
Headland Place field strip [2].19
health [8].19
  doctors [11].76, 78-85, 87
  medicine [11].79, 81-2
Health Association [12].15
Hearle, T. W. [8].31, 32
Hearth Tax [3].11; [4].19; [5].4;
    [11].69
hearths [10].12, 13
Heaviside, John [11].80-1, 83
Hedges, John [7].22
hedging and ditching [6].6; [9].15
Hedgings, J. [8].20
Hell Ley field [4].21
Hell Wood [4].*4*
Hemel Hempstead [1].5; [6].27
Hempsall school [8].*30*, 32
Henry II, King [6].10
Henry III, King [4].9
Henry VII, King [7].7
Henry VIII, King [1].16, 17, 18-19;
    [2].8; [4].17; [6].9;
    [7].5, 7, 10; [11].59
Herne Hill [5].21
Hertford [3].28; [9].40; [11].9, 67
  Assizes [6].18-19; [11].64
  and inns [3].29, 30
  market [9].16
  paper mill [11].69
  pubs [3].29, 30
  railway [5].16, *17*, 21, 23, 26
  shops [4].26; [8].21
  in WWI [12].7

Hertford Bridewell [6].17
Hertford Castle [4].8
Hertford Flyer [5].23
Hertford Gaol [6].21
Hertford Hospital [8].19
Hertford Mercury [6].23-4; [11].41
Hertford North [5].16, *17*, 23
Hertford Quarter Sessions [3].5; [6].10
Hertford Rural Deanery [7].5
Hertford and Welwyn Junction Railway [5].16
Hertfordshire [9].19
Hertfordshire Agricultural Society [9].34, 40
Hertfordshire Constabulary *see* County Police Force
Hertfordshire County Council [2].31; [4].20; [9].41; [11].60
    Education Committee [8].14
    and roads [5].30
    schools [4].24; [7].12; [8].15, 19, 30, 32
    listed [8].32
Hertfordshire County Press [6].18
Hertfordshire Diocese [7].5
Hertfordshire Militia [11].38, 43
Hertfordshire Show [8].17
Hertingfordbury [5].16, *17*, 23; [11].57, 59
Herts Advertiser and St. Albans Times [7].26
Herts Mercury [11].78
Herts Mercury and General Advertiser [9].33
Hetherington, James [3].29
Hetherington, Thomas [3].29
Hewinson (overseer) [9].16
Hickinbottom, Sam [2].25
Hickson family [11].54
    Hickson, Emily [11].34
    Hickson, Sarah Sophia [11].34
    Hickson, Thomas [11].34

hides [1].20, *20*, 23, 24; [2].4-5, 8; [6].5
higgler [11].88
Higgs, William [3].21
High Street *see* Fore Street
Highefield [2].16
Highway Duty [9].18
highwaymen [3].27-8; [11].64
Hill family [2].24; [11].27, 54
    Hill, A. C. [9].44
    Hill, Anthony [7].22
    Hill, Elizabeth [11].56
    Hill, George [7].22
    Hill, Helen [11].56
    Hill, John [7].21
    Hill, Lucy [8].20
    Hill, Mr. (builder) [2].31
    Hill, Nicholas [11].55, 56, 57
    Hill, Thomas [2].12; [11].56
    Hill, William, Senior [11].55, 56
    Hill, William (*d.1593*) [11].56
    Hill (of Roe Green North Farm) [2].15, 16-17
Hill End Farm [9].47
Hill End Hospital [5].23
Hill Farm [9].*24*
Hill House [2].25; [4].18, 19; [10].28; [11].36, 40, 84, *84*
    OS grid ref. [10].31
Hill Ley [2].32
Hilltop (Hill Top) [2].24; [12].22
    Community Centre [2].*cover*
    pub [3].*16*, 22, 30
Hillyer, Rev. Norman [4].24
Hilyer, Mary [8].26-7
Hind, James [3].28
Hindley, Brig. [12].25-6
Hine, D. [7].22
Hine, Reginald [8].5
Hinsley, Cardinal [7].29
Hinton, John [11].67
Hipgrave family [2].30; [11].54
Hitchin [5].*10*, *11*, 12, 13, 18, 21, *22*, 23; [6].15, 27; [9].34

Hixon, Widow [2].30
Hodge's shop [10].28
Hoding, Geoffrey [1].22
Hoding, William [1].22; [11].77
Holden, William [3].12
Hollier, Mr. (of Roe Green South
    Farm) [2].17, 19
Holliers Dairy [6].25
Hollier's (Hill's) Farm [2].15
Holliers Way [2].32
Hollingsworth, Mary [11].56
Hollingsworth, William [3].29;
    [11].17
Holly Bush messuage [11].31
Holly Bush pub, Hatfield Hyde
    [3].*16*, 21, 30
Holly Bush pub, Park Street [3].*8*,
    30; [11B].*cover*
Holly Cottages [2].14, 25, 27;
    [10].*23*
    OS grid ref. [10].31
    plan [10].*22, 22*
Holly Field [2].21
Hollybush shops [12].12
Holmes, Sir Robert [8].8
Holstok, William [10].6
Holt-White, Rev. [8].27-8
Holwell [1].*6*, 16
    farms [9].6, 7, 18, 20, 21, 22,
        29, 32, 37, 44, 46
Holwell Hyde (Holwellhyde) [1].*20*;
    [4].*26*; [11].59
Holwell Manor [1].22; [7].22;
    [9].29; [10].9, 21;
    [11].40
    OS grid ref. [10].31
Holwell Mill [1].12
Holy Lamb Inn [3].31
Home Farm (Lawn Farm) [1].*8, 9,*
    10, 17; 4,20, 22; [9].16-
    18, 21, *24*, 48; [11].31,
    36
Homestead Court Hotel [12].22
Hoote, E. [7].26

Hopcraft, Miss (Headmistress)
    [8].32
Hopfields [7].20
    pub [3].*16*, 20, 30
hops [3].6; [11].18
Hopgrounds field [3].20
Horn family [9].14, 31, 41; [11].58-
    60
    Horn, J. B. [11].58
    Horn, Sarah [11].16
    Horn, W. C. (of Handside) [9].3,
        14, 45; [11].29; [12].*4*
    Horn, W. J. [9].30
    Horn, William Cooper (*b.1810*)
        [11].16
    Horn, William James [9].41;
        [11].16, 60
hornbeam [1].27
Hornbeam (Hornebeame) Hall
    [3].21; [11].57, 58
Hornbeam Lane [4].6
Hornbeamgate Manor [1].*20*; [2].8;
    [4].3-4, 16, 17, 21; [9].7
Horne, Francis [11].14
Hornet, Phoebe [8].23
Hornsey [5].19, *22*
Horse and Groom alehouse, Fore
    Street [3].*8*, 23, 30;
    [11].6, *12*, 24
Horse and Groom inn, Park Street
    [3].*8*, 15, 30
Horse and Groom (Horse and
    Jockey), Stanborough
    [3].13, 29
Horse and Jockey [3].29
horses
    on farms [9].18, 19
    hiring [11].88
    names [9].27
    stabling [9].39
    theft of [6].22
    tolls [1].11
    on trains [5].21
    in war [12].7

32

Horseshoes pub [11].42
Horsey, Edward William [11].29, 34
Horsey, Fanny [11].30, 85
Horsey, Frances, school [8].*30*, 31
Horsey, Mary Ann Frances [11].34
Horsey, William [11].25
horticulture [9].22, 48
Hospitallers of St. John of God [7].30
hospitals
   Tolmers [4].20, 25
   V. A. D. [8].25; [12].7
   WGC [12].15
Hossman, Thomas [4].24
hotels [3].9
   see also names
Houghton (later Bottomley), Betty [8].13, 29
Houghton (Salisbury's agent) [7].11
House of Correction [6].8, 15, 16, 19
houseboot [1].16; [10].5
houses [10].**5-32**
   Aldykes [10].*cover*, 24-5, 30
   cottages [10].**21-5**
      see also separate entry
   Council houses [1].7; [9].45; [10].29
   damp [12].24
   farm houses [10].**12-21**
   larger houses [10].**8-11**
   Malting Mead terrace [2].31; [3].9
   materials [10].**5-8**
   19th c. [11].41
   ownership [11].7
   timber-framed [1].19; [10].5, 10, 12
   town houses [10].**25-30**
   storm damage [12].24-5, *24*
   WGC [12].**9-11**, *10*
   see also names
How Croft [1].*18*
Howard, Dan [3].*22*
Howard, Ebenezer [12].8
Howard, Will [3].23-4
Howe, Edward [6].17
Howe, William [3].26
Howe (How) Dell [1].*8, 9, 13, 18*; [2].21; [5].16; [9].18, 19; [7].9
   sub-soil [1].26
Howe Dell (How Dell) School [1].17; [7].9; [8].4, 32; [10].11
Howe Grove [2].16
Howe Wood [4].16
Howes, Mr. (preacher) [7].16
Howlands Farm [9].*cover*, 5
Hoy, Edward [11].*12*, 39-40
Hudson, Elizabeth [11].26
Hugh Fitz Simon [6].10
Hugh le Brun [4].9
Hughes, John [6].17
Hughes, Michael [12].3
Hulks family [2].25, 31; [11].43, 54
   Hulks, Arthur [8].21
   Hulks, Dorothy [11].43
   Hulks, Eliza [11].42
   Hulks, James [3].26; [11].42
   Hulks, Job [11].43
   Hulks, John [11].42, 43
   Hulks, Joseph [11].42
   Hulks, Maria [2].25; [11].43
   Hulks, Maria Lydia [11].42
   Hulks, Samuel [8].21
   Hulks, Sarah [11].42
   Hulks, Sarah Ann [11].42
   Hulks, William [2].25; [9].16; [11].42, 43
   Hulks, William John [11].42
Hundred Court [6].10
hundreds [6].5, 10; [11].57
Hunt, Mrs. (conveyor) [6].15
Hunt, Rev. J. B. [7].19
Hunter family [9].5
   Hunter, John (from Glasgow) [9].3, 5, 37-8, 45
   Hunter, John (of Hitchin) [9].34
   Hunter, M. [8].21

Hunter, Mr. (of Peartree) [9].40
Hunters Bridge [5].13
hunting [1].15; [4].6; [9].30
Huntingdon [5].5, *11*
   Archdeacon [7].21
Huntman, Joseph [3].30; [11].61
Husband, Azariah [8].7
Hutchin, Dr. Kenneth [11].13, 83
Hutchinson, Mr. (of Woodhall)
   [9].23; [11].76
Hutton, Barbara
   author Parts [1], [10] *and* [12]
Hutton, Kenneth B.
   author Part [5]
Hyll, Johanna [6].7
Hyll, Nicholas [6].7
Hylle family [2].12

I

I Was a Spy (film) [12].15
ice-cap [1].27
Illustrated London News [5].13, 14
immorality and morals [5].11; [6].7; [7].15; [11].70
implements [9].18
imports [8].7
Improved Public House Co. [3].29
Indells [2].32
Industrial Revolution [9].23
industrialisation [12].16
Ingram family [11].9
   Ingram, Henry [11].9
inmates [6].11
innkeepers *see* publicans
inns [1].10; [3].9-22; [11].87
   arrangement [3].12
   bibliography [3].3
   charges [3].9
   early [3].4-5
   1824 [9].30
   1850 [5].13
   and Great North Road [5].8, 9
   in literature [3].26-8
   listed [3].29-32
   opening hours [3].5, 18
   smaller [3].15-22
   trade tokens [3].14, *15*
   see also inn names; pubs
inn signs [3].4, 15, 19
Inspectors [8].8, 20, 26-9
insurance [3].14; [6].15; [11].88
   health [12].6
inventories [9].10; [10].10
   1603, of yeoman's widow
   [9].11
   1682, of yeoman [9].12
   1717, of farmer [9].13
   1724, of collar-maker [11].18-19
   1726, of shop-keeper [11].19-21
   1770, of farmer [11].32
   1869, of shop-keeper [11].44-5
Ireland, Jesper [7].21
Ireland, John [3].30
Ireland, Timothy [3].30
Irish labourers [5].14
Iron Room [7].17-18
ironmongers [11].73, 87
irrigation [9].23
Irwin, Edward Ingram, 4th Viscount [11].9
Irwin, Lord (President of Board of Education) [8].15
Irwine, Arthur Ingram, 3rd Viscount [2].13, 17
Isabel of Angoulême [4].9
Isgate, Anne and Gertrude [8].23
Ismailia cottage [2].31
Ivery, Edward and Ann [11].10
Ives, John [3].11
Ivory, Nicholas [11].57
Ivy Cottage [6].24

J

J. J. Burgess and Son [11].39
Jack Olding's corner [1].4, 5, 11
Jackson, Abraham [7].22
Jackson, John [11].27
Jackson, M. A. [8].27
Jackson, Mr. (advertiser) [11].41

Jacobs (Jacob's) Well pub [3].*8*, 15, 26, 30; [5].13
James I, King [1].11-12, 16
James II, King [7].4, 8
James, Anthony [3].23
James, Charles [6].17
James, James [6].17
James, John [6].6
Jehovah's Witnesses [7].31
Jemys, John [6].6
Jessett, George [11].25
Jesshop, E. S. [11].35
Jews [9].16
Joane de Monchensy [4].9
John, King [4].9
John atte Byrches [1].22
John atte Greene [2].24
John atte Hill [2].24
John de Blomvil [6].10
John de Canvil [1].21, 22
John de la Wyle [1].21
John de Molys [6].10
John de Ponsbourne [4].7
John de Stoke [2].8, 24
John de Valence [4].9
John the hayward [4].16
Johnson family [11].59, 64-5
    Johnson, Henry (brickmaker, d.*1718*) [11].7, 16, 36, 64-5
    Johnson, Henry (Dissenter) [7].21
    Johnson, Henry (yeoman, d.*1730)* [11].15, 16, 18, 19, 38
    Johnson, John [11].19, 65
    Johnson, Miss (Headmistress) [8].32
    Johnson, Samuel [6].17
    Johnson, Sarah [11].59
    Johnson, Thomas [6].13; [11].6, 15, 19
    Johnson, William [11].25
Jones, John [6].15
Jones, Thomas [11].64
Jordan, Joseph [3].30
Joseph, Sir Keith [12].22

Joy, Rev. Joseph [7].24
Justices of the Peace [3].5; [6].10, 11-14, 15-16, 28; [11].5

K

K.C.V. Precision Tool Co. [8].11, 26
Karron, Rev. J. [8].19
Keepers of the Peace [6].10
Keet (Keats, Keit), Rev. John (Rector *1752-63*) [7].12, 13, 14-15
J. P. [9].16
Keet (Keate), Rev. John (Rector *1788-1819*) [7].12, 13
    farming [9].20, 21
Kelly, Eustace [11].63
Kelly's Directory [8].9, 22; [11].41
    1839 [8].10
Kelshall [5].6
Kempster, Thomas [3].5; [6].13
Kennington, Eric [3].15
Kentish family [11].52
    Kentish, Benjamin [11].40
    Kentish, Solomon [11].40
Kentish Lane Farm [1].*15*; [9].9, *25*; [10].19
    OS grid ref. [10].31
Kiff, Sam [2].30
Kilby, William [6].13
Kill Devil field [4].21
kiln [2].*18*
    brick kiln [9].18
    lime kiln [2].21
Kimpton [11].61
Kimpton, Mary [11].*12*, 16
Kimpton, Sarah [11].34
Kimpton, Thomas [11].*12*, 19
King's Arms [3].31
King's Cross [5].4, 19, 21, 23, 25
King's Head (formerly Maidenhead) inn [3].*8*, 14, 31; [10].28; [11].*12*, 19, 22, 65, 81
    OS grid ref. [10].31

Kingsbury Brewery [3].6; [11].11
Kirby, William [6].21
Kircher, Robert, DD [2].10
Kirkham, J. E. [8].32
Kitchen, John [7].10
kitchens [10].21
Knebworth [5].21, 26
Knella Road [12].12
Knighton, Ann [4].12
Knightsfield [12].12
Kybe, William [1].21
Kybes Green [1].21

L

Labour Party [12].13
laceman [11].55, 70
Lacey, Rev. T. W. [7].24, 25
Lamb family [11].52
    Lamb, Henry [11].35
    Lamb, Matthew (of Lincoln's Inn) [8].5
    Lamb, Sir Matthew (of Brocket Park) [2].13
Lamb inn [3].31
Lambert, Nancy [7].25
Land, John [7].21
land surveys [9].46-8
land tax [11].7, 33
Land Terrier, *1855* [9].28, 31, 32, 37
land use [9].19, 45-6
    agricultural *see* arable land
Land Utilization Survey [9].19
landholders, *1251* [4].7
landlords
    Newgate Street [4].7
    town [11].7-11
    see also publicans
Lane End [2].32
Langland, William [3].26
Langton family [3].24
Lankford, John G. [3].18, 24
larceny (burglary, theft) [6].7, 17, 18-19, 21, 22

Larence, John [11].69
Latin [6].5; [8].4
Lattimore, Mrs. (publican) [3].29
Lattimore, William [3].29
Lawn Farm *see* Home Farm
Lawn House [8].5-6; [11].67
Lawrence family [3].25; [11].54
    Lawrence, George [3].25
    Lawrence, James [3].26
    Lawrence, Sidney Christmas [11].26
    Lawrence, Thomas [3].25
Lawrence de Thebrege [4].6
Lawrence Hall [7].*20*, 31
Lawrie, Mrs. (schoolmistress) [8].28
lawyers [11].78-9
Le Hay house [2].16
le Paum, William [4].7
Lea, River *see* River Lea
Lea valley [1].27; [4].25; [5].9, 27
Lea Valley Growers' Association [4].25
Lea Valley swimming pool [1].4
lead [10].7
Leake, Sir John [3].29
Leaper, John [7].21
leather [6].6; [11].20, 21
Lee, Dr. Richard [7].11
Lee, William [11].65
Leech, Jonas [6].11
Legg, William [11].29
Leggs [9].*24*; [11].61
    Charity Land [9].5
    Farm [9].29
Leicester, Bishops of [7].5
Leicester, Robert Dudley, Earl of [4].18, 19
Leigh, William [11].39
Lemsford [1].6, *6*, 22, *25*; [9].16, 46, 48; [11].60; [12].26
    church [5].8; [7].16, 21, 26
    Cottage [10].21
    OS grid ref. [10].31
    plan [10].*22*

farms [9].6, 30, 44; [11].58
Mill [1].11, 24; [2].4, 14; [3].9;
   [5].7; [6].22
   worship at [7].22
pubs [3].13, 15, 20-1, 23, 24, 31
School [8].*30*, 31
Lemsford Road [1].11, *14*
bungalows [9].43
cottages [10].24; [12].5
railway platform [5].7, 23
Leonard, Rev. Martin Patrick
   Grange [7].12
L'Estrange Malone, Mrs. [12].21
level crossings [1].10; [5].15-16
Lewer, Martin [11].14
Lewer, Tite [11].14
Lewis, S.: *Topographical Directory*
   [5].13
Lewis, William [11].76
Leyland, Harriet [8].31
Leyland, John [8].31
libraries [12].6
   County [12].22
   Public [8].*30*, 31
   Rural [12].6
licences [3].4, 15, 18; [6].13, 14
lime, price [10].25
limeburners [11].65
Lime Kiln [2].*20*
Lincoln [5].13; [7].5, 10
literature [3].26-8
Little Berkhamsted [4].10, 17, 22, 24
Little Dell [2].21
Little Ease field [4].21
Little Naste Hyde [2].*18*
Little Park [1].*15*
Liverpool [5].9
Lizard (Lizards) Lane [3].10; [11].6, *12*
Lloyd family [3].6; [9].31, 43
   Lloyd, Doreen [8].32
   Lloyd, Roger [5].28
Lloyd Thomas, Dr. William [11].82

L. N. W. Railway [5].18, 26
Local Government Act *1888* [6].25
lock-up [11].*12*
Lockwood, Sammell [9].16
Lodewikhide [2].*20*
Lodge School [8].11
lodgekeepers [11].88
lodging houses [11].87
Log Books, schools [8].16-26
Logsdell, Elizabeth [11].18-19
Logsdell, Robert [11].18
Logsdon, Edward [11].35
Lokke, John [6].4, 20; [10].6
Lombard Street [11].55
London [5].5-6, 7; [9].19, 36
   bombing [12].17
   City [11].54-5, 70, 75
   expansion [12].8
   markets [9].17, 21, 22, 27, 28,
      35, 36, 37, 38, 42, 45
   Metropolitan Police [6].22
   railway [5].13, 14, 18, 19, 21, 22
      Round-London Railway
         [5].18
   refuse from [5].23
London and North Western Railway
   [5].*10*
London and Northern Railway
   [5].*11*
London and York Railway [5].*11*, 12, 26
London Auction Mart [3].7
London Chronicle [3].23
London Colney [12].17
London Diocese [7].5
London Evening Post [3].10
London Mail [11].77
London Road *see* Great North Road
London Road School [8].*cover*, 9,
   11-13, *12*, *30*, 31; [8].9;
   [11].38
   expenses [8].11
   inspectors' report [8].26-9

37

Object Lessons [8].28
and New Towns [12].8, 18-19,
20-1
Long, Edmund [11].*12*, 25, 34
Long, Sarah [11].34
Long Arm and Short Arm pub
[3].15, *16*, 20, 25, 31
Long Brache (Longbreach)
Common Field [2].15,
18
Long Pain field [4].21
Longcroft Field [1].12, 13; [2].16
Longfield [6].19
Longmore, P. E. [12].21
Longstaff family [11].79-80
  Longstaff, Ann [11].80
  Longstaff, John [11].80
  Longstaff, William [11].80
Longstaffe, John [11].11
Longway cottage [2].31
Loop Line [5].*10*
Lord of the Manor [1].15-17, 19;
[5].13; [6].6, 8-9, 11
La Rothe Hide [2].4-5, 14, *20*
Louth family [2].8; [9].7
Louthes manor [2].8
Lowe, G. R. [12].21
Lowen, James [11].25, 83
Lower Handside Farm [9].41;
[11].60
Lower Woodside
  farm [1].15; [9].9, *24*, 44
  hamlet [1].*13*
Lowthes Chantry [11].8
Lucas, Dr. Carr Ellison [11].81, 82
Lucas, Henrietta [11].81
Lucas, Richard [2].20
Lucy family [4].12
  Lucy, Sir Edmund [4].12
  Lucy, Henry [4].12
Ludford family [11].62
  Ludford, Henry [11].62
  Ludford, Nicholas [11].62, 80
Ludlow [6].14
Ludwick [12].22

farms [9].6, 7
Manor [9].7
shops [12].12
Ludwick Arms pub [3].*17*, 21, 31
Ludwick Hall [9].*24*; [10].9, 11, 19;
[11].60
OS grid ref. [10].310
Ludwick Hide (Ludwickhyde)
[4].*26*; [9].12, 29
farm rooms [9].10
Ludwick Way [7].20
Ludwickhyde Ward [11].59, 60, 69
Luffanhide [9].6
Luton [5].*17*, 18, 19, 21, 23
Luton and Dunstable branch line
[5].18-19, 23, 26
Luton, Dunstable and Welwyn Co.
[5].18
Lyon inn [3].11-12, *11*, 31
see also White Lion

M

M.1 road [9].46
MacDonnell, J. H. [12].21
Machell family [2].13; [11].8-9
  Machell, John [11].8
machinery [9].20, 39
Mackay, Dugald [9].3, 44, 46
MacKay, G. W. S. [8].32
Mackay, Willie [9].44, 46
Macky, Robert [3].30
Maddock, Rev. E. J. [4].3
Madeley, Joseph [11].56
Madeley, Sarah [11].56, 57
magistrates [11].46
Maiden Head (Maidenhead, King's
Head) inn [3].31;
[11].19, 22
Mail Coaches [11].76
malt [11].6
malt-houses [3].5-6
malting [3].5-6
Malting Mead terrace houses [2].31;
[3].9
maltings [3].*8*, 9; [8].11; [11].36-8

maltsters [11].10, *12*, 36-8, 87
Manchester [5].9, *11*, 26, 27
Manfield family [3].9
　Manfield, Benjamin [11].65
Manfield Berner Malting [3].*8*
Manlove, John [11].5
Mann, Crossman & Paulin [3].31
Mannynge, Henry [11].63
Mannynge, Robert [11].63
Manor Court [3].14, 19; [6].5-9, 10,
　　11, 20; [11].24, 57, 59
manor courts [1].23
Manor Farm [1].17
manor-houses [10].9-11
　(preceding old Palace) [10].6, 7
Manor Road [11].66
Manor Rolls [3].19
Manse [7].25
mantua-maker [11].87
manure [9].21, 22-3, 27, 36, 37, 43,
　　45
Maple Bank house [10].7
maps [1].3; [2].3
　early settlements [1].*25*
　early place names [2].*20*
　mediaeval Great Wood [1].*15*
　mediaeval sub-manor and hides
　　[1].*20*
　1603 open fields [1].*13, 14*
　17c. farm boundaries [2].7
　1777 [2].*28*
　1780 [11].8, 12
　1796 Hatfield Hyde [9].6
　1824 [9].28-30
　　farm names [9].*24-5*
　1829 Common Fields [2].*18*
　1838 tithe map [9].*31-3*
　1848 [1].*9*
　1852 [1].*8*; [2].*20*; [3].*8*; [5].*10*
　1921 [1].*6*
　1950 railways [5].*17*
　1959 [1].*5*; [2].6; [3].16-17;
　　[5].*32*
　1961 [4].*4*; [11].*50*
　1962 [7].*20, 27*; [8].*30*

modern street plan [2].*6*
natural features [1].26
Newgate Street [4].*26*
Ordnance Survey, *1961 op.*
　　[11].49; *op.* [12].1
Mardall, George [11].10, 38
Mardell family [11].54
Mardling family [2].30; [11].54
Market Gardens [9].43, 48
Market House [6].21; [8].10, *10*, 11;
　　[11].*cover*, 5, 6, *12*, 54
Market Place [11].*cover*
Market Square [8].10
markets [5].19; [11].4-6, 46
　cattle [9].33
　Hertford [9].16
　London [9].17, 19, 21, 22, 27,
　　28, 35, 36, 37, 38, 42,
　　45
　Newgate Street [4].7
　St. Albans [9].36
　tolls [11].5, 73
Marks and Spencer [12].12
Marlborough Almshouses [11].68
Marlborough, George Spencer, 5th
　　Duke of [9].29
Marley Hall [7].*20*, 31
marling (chalk) [2].21; [9].14
Marquis of Granby pub [3].30
marriage
　banns [11].5
　bigamy [6].17
Marsh, Mr. (farmer) [9].20, 21, 22
Marshall (architect) [9].43
Marshall, John (pub owner) [3].31
Marshall, Mary [3].32
Marshall, Thomas [6].16
Marshallsheath [9].14
Marsham, Thomas [11].75
Marshmoor farm [3].24
Marshmoor Lane [5].8, 16, *17*
Marston, John [4].18-19
Marten, Ambrose [9].11
Martin, James [9].10
Martin, Jon [9].10

39

Martin of Methelwold [1].22
Mary I, Queen [1].16; [4].17
Maryland [2].32
Maslen (Maslem), Rev. Charles [7].23, 25; [11].25, 32
Mason, Mary [2].25
Masters, F. H. [12].*4*
Matthews, Betty [8].32
Matthews, H. L. R. [12].21
Matthews, Richard [11].19-20
   inventory [11].20-1
Mawe, Harry [11].77
Mawe, John [11].77
Mawe, Mary [11].77
Mawe, Ruth [11].77
Maxwell-Fry, Mr. [12].26
May, William [7].10
Maybank, William [6].17
Maynard, C. G. [12].21, 25
Mazawattee Tea [11].18
McComb, J. E. [12].21, 25
McCowan (agent) [9].42
McMullen, Peter [3].21
McMullen & Sons [3].22, 29, 30, 31, 32
measles [8].18, 19
Medcalf, T. D. [3].30
Medical Club [12].6, 15
medicine [11].79, 81-2
   doctors [11].76, 78-85, 87
Melbourne, Elizabeth, Lady [9].20
Melbourne, William Lamb, 2nd Viscount [2].13, 32; [9].30; [11].54, 58, 82
   inns owned by [3].29, 31
Mery, Philip [6].6
Methodist and Wesleyan chapels and churches [7].**25-7**
   Birchwood [7].*27*, 30, 31
   French Horn Lane [3].19; [7].17, 26-7
   Moo-cow Chapel [7].26, *27*, 31
   Newgate Street [4].23
   Oxlease [7].*27*, 31
   Sleapshyde [7].26

and Toleration Act [7].22
WGC [7].*20*, 31
Methodists *see* Protestant Dissenters
Metropolitan Police [6].22
Michells Farm [2].16
Middle Park [1].*13*, *15*, *18*, *20*; [4].*26*
Middlesex [6].14
Mid-Herts College of Further Education [12].26
Midland Railway [5].*10*, 18, 26
migration [11].53
Mildmay, Sir Walter [2].10
milestones [2].*28*; [5].18
Militia [8].17, 18
   Barracks [11].74
   Return [11].76, 86, 87, 88
   Roll [5].4
milk
   in diet [12].14
   price [9].28
   for schools [8].25
Milkwell field [1].17, [9].9
Mill Green [1].12, *26*, 26, 27; [2].22, 32
   farms [9].6, 7, 23, 34, 40; [11].71
   mills [1].24; [6].17, *18*; [11].69-71
   pubs [3].10, *16*, 26, *26*, 30; [11].71
Millard, John [6].13, 14
Miller, Elizabeth [11].10
Miller, Ganzelius [11].77
millers [11].59, 61-71, 86; [11].26
Miller's Field [2].19
Millers Park *see* Milward's Park
milliners [2].30; [8].23; [11].87
millinery [5].18, 19; [11].22
Millington, Gerald V. [4].3-4; [11].52
   author Part [4]
mills [11].61, 69-70
   Creswick's [11].70
   fulling [6].11, 17; [11].69

grain [6].17; [11].69, 70-1
Manor [11].69
oil [11].70
paper [5].13; [6].17, *18*; [9].*24*;
   [11].69-70
Pickford [11].70
silk [5].13
water [1].24; [6].11
see also names of mills
Mills family [4].25
  Mills (publican) [3].32
  Mills, John Remington [4].20
  Mills, Samuel [4].20
  Mills, Thomas, M.P. [4].20, 23, 24; [7].15
Mills Farm, The [9].32
Milward's (Middle, Millers, Millwards) Park [1].*6*, 14; [2].*28*; [5].8, *32*; [9].*24*
  concrete wall [10].8
  OS grid ref. [10].31
  farming [9].16, 33
  houses [10].6
  and roads [1].4, 5, 8, 9, 9-10, 11, *15*; [5].8, *32*
Milne, Fr. [7].29
Milne Green [6].11
Mimms Hall [4].10
Mims Field [2].*20*
Ministry of Transport [5].30
Minster Close [2].*6*, 32
Mission Hall [2].31
Mission Rooms [7].17-19, *19*, 31
Missionary Society [7].28
Mitchell, Leonard [11].38
Mitchell, Mary [11].38
Mitchell, Richard [2].16
Mitchell's Malting [11].*12*, 38
Mitre (Rose and Crown) alehouse [3].31; [11].27
Moat [2].8; [4].4, 6
Mold Co. Flint [6].15
Mole Field [2].21
Molesworth, Agnes Maria [11].85

monasteries [3].4; [6].11
Monday's Park [10].12
Monk, E. [4].3
Monken Hadley [11].69
'Moo-cow Chapel' [7].26, *27*, 31
Moorcroft, Benjamin [7].22
Moore family [11].13, 54, 69-70
  Moore, Andrew [4].19
  Moore, Charles [12].12
  Moore, Isaac [11].*12*, 69
morals and immorality [5].11; [6].7; [7].15; [11].70
More family [2].10
  More, Alicia [6].9
  More, Basil [2].12
  More, John [4].10
  More, Sir John [2].9; [6].9
  More, Sir Thomas [1].18; [2].9, *9*, 32; [6].9
Morgan, Pierpont [4].14
Morgan, William [6].16
Morning Chronicle [3].27
Morrall Hill (Morrell Hill)
  brickyards [10].7; [11].63, 64, 65
Morrell, Hugh [6].11
Morrell, Walter [6].11, 17; [11].69
Morris, Hannah [11].16
Morton, John, Bishop (later Cardinal) [1].19; [7].7; [10].7
Morton (poacher) [6].19
Morton House, Fore Street [8].32; [10].27-8; [11].11, 13, 66, 83
  OS grid ref. [10].32
Morton's Palace *see* Old Palace
Moryson, Charles [4].11
Mosquito aircraft [12].17
Mothers' Meeting [12].6
Moul, William [11].43, 44
Mount Pleasant [1].11
Mousley, Margaret [4].20
Mud Chapel [7].16
"Mud Modes" (cartoon) [5].20

Munday family [11].54
Municipal Housing Acts [1].7
Murphy Radio [12].15
Murray family [9].44
Mushroom Field [9].27
music
   organist [11].88
   Prykking Song [2].12; [6].4,
     [6].7
   schools [8].31, 32
Musman, E. B. [3].14-15
Muswell Hill [8].25
Mychylle croft [2].10
Myhill (fellmonger) [11].29
Mylles, John [2].27
Mymsfield [2].10

N

Naden family [11].54
   Naden, John (builder) [2].11, 27;
     [11].42
   Naden, John (plumber, b.*1817*)
     [11].38, 42
   Naden, John (plumber, b.*1854*)
     [11].38, 42
Naden's builders yard [3].9
Nags Head [3].30
names [1].21
   family [2].**24-5**
   farms [9].**5-6**, 32
   field [2].16, **19-21**, *20*
   Hatfield [1].24
   street [2].**32**
   surnames [1].20, 21-2
Napoleonic Wars [9].26; [11].59
Nash family [11].43, 54
   Nash, Thomas [6].17
Nashes Farm [9].41
Nast Hyde [5].*17*; [7].28
   Farm [2].17, *18*; [9].29
Naste Field [1].12, *13*
National Health Insurance [12].15
National Omnibus Company [5].30

National Schools [8].9-15
   boys [8].10-11, 12, 13, *13*, 14
   Endymion Road [8].13, *14*
   in Fore Street [8].10, 11, *30*, 31
   girls [8].11, 12, 13-14
   infants [8].11
     see also London Road School
   Lodge School [8].11
   Log Books [8].16-26
   Parsonage Drive [8].11
   Puttocks Oak [8].11, 12, *30*, 31
     see also St. Audrey's School
National Society for Promoting the
   Education ... [8].10, 11
National Union of Railwaymen
   [8].13-14
natural resources [1].27
Neale, Sir John [4].11
   The Elizabethan House of
     Commons [4].11
Neale, William [11].*12*, 27
Nelseam, Robert [6].7
Nelson, Roger [4].23
New Barnet [5].26
New Fiddle pub [2].*18*, 27, 31;
   [3].*16*, 21-2, 31
New Field [2].19, 27
New, Keith [12].24
New Park [4].9, 21-2; [9].32
New Park farm [1].*15*; [4].21; [9].9,
   25, 46, 47
New Park Road [4].21, 25, 26
New Pond [8].17
New Road [1].11; [5].9
New Town (Hatfield) [1].4, 5, 6, *6*,
   22; [2].12, 13; [11].3,
   58; [12].6
   building, *1848* [11].41
   churches [7].18, 27, 29
   farming [9].18, 42, 48
   houses [10].8, 29
   lawbreaking [6].28
   population [5].4, 5; [7].30

shops **[11]**.33
tradesmen **[11]**.43-6
   families pedigree **[11]**.42
New Town (WGC) **[1]**.5; **[12]**.19-22
   farming **[9]**.42
New Town Commission **[12]**.25
   see also Development
   Corporations
New Town Plan **[12]**.19, *23*
New Towns **[12]**.16, 18-20, 25
New Towns Act **[5]**.4; **[10]**.30;
   [12].19, 20
Newcastle **[5]**.*11*
Newgate **[4]**.6
Newgate Hyde **[3]**.5
Newgate Street (Newgatestreet,
   Newgayt Strate) **[1]**.*6,
   15*, 20; **[4]**.**3-4, 5-26**
   churches **[4]**.23-4; **[7]**.15, 30
   farms **[4]**.21-3; **[9]**.4, *25*
   landholders chart **[4]**.*7*
   map **[4]**.*4*
   pubs **[3]**.29, 30; **[4]**.23
   railway **[4]**.24-5
   schools **[4]**.24; **[8]**.31
   segregated as separate parish
     [4].24
   in WWII **[4]**.26
Newgate Street Ward **[6]**.12
Newman, Arthur **[11]**.26
Newman, John **[6]**.6
Newman, John Henry **[7]**.21
Newman, Martha **[11]**.85
Newpark Farm **[4]**.*4*, 5
newsagent **[11]**.87
Newstead **[2]**.3
Newtown ("California") **[1]**.7;
   [11].3, 41, 43, 78
   church **[7]**.17, 24-5
   houses **[10]**.28
   Police **[5]**.14
   pubs **[3]**.21-3
   and railway **[6]**.24
   shops **[12]**.12-13

Newtown Brewery **[3]**.7, 8, 18
Newtown House **[1]**.7; **[11]**.66;
   [12].13, *21*; **[8]**.32
Newtown School **[1]**.7; **[8]**.25, 30;
   [9].43; **[11]**.66
Niccoll, Francis Carter **[11]**.10
Nicholas, John **[7]**.22
Nicholasson, Alexander **[6]**.4
Nicholls, Emily Ann **[11]**.30
Nicholls, Samuel **[6]**.13, 14
Nicklay Field **[2]**.*20*
Nightingall family **[11]**.61-2
   Nightingall, John **[11]**.62
   Nightingall, Walter J. **[11]**.62
Nock, OS: *The Great Northern
   Railway* **[5]**.25
Nomansland Common **[11]**.55
Nonconformist Churches **[7]**.21-5
Nonconformist Ministers *see*
   Antrobus, Rev. J. K.;
   Bird, Rev. John Cox;
   Broady, Rev. William;
   Buzza, Rev. W.A.;
   Cheeseman, Rev. T.;
   Crow, Rev. T.; Garlick,
   Rev. G.; Joy, Rev.
   Joseph; Lacey, Rev. T.
   W.; Maslen, Rev.
   Charles; Packer, Rev.
   G.; Raban, Rev. Samuel;
   Raven, Rev.; Sherrell,
   Rev.
Norfolk **[10]**.7
Norman Conquest **[1]**.23-4; **[2]**.4
Norman, Mr. (gardener) **[8]**.18
Norman, Mrs. A. M. **[8]**.18, 32
Norman, William (tailor) **[11]**.*12*
North Eastern Railway (N. E. R.)
   [5].11, 26
North London Railway **[5]**.21
North Mymms (Mimms) **[1]**.18;
   [12].11
   boundary **[2]**.4
   church **[7]**.29
   Currell family **[11]**.54

farms [9].18, 38
   Toll Gate Farm [9].*35*
Gubbins [2].9
Parsonage [2].21, *28*
North Mymms Field [2].10
North Orbital Road [2].14; [5].7, 18
North Place [1].10; [11].71, 81, 82, 83
North Road (old) [3].9-10, 13, 14, 15, 20; [8].31
   see also Great North Road
Northampton [9].14
Northaw [6].28; [7].29, 30; [12].11
Northaw Great Wood [1].*15*; [4].5
Northcotts [1].10; [9].13; [11].9, 40; [12].7
Northcotts house [11].81
Northcotts school [8].30, [8].31
Northwold, Hugh [7].6, 9
Northwold, Nicholas [7].6
Norton Grinding Wheels [12].15
Nunn, Henry [11].11, *12*
nurseries [4].25

O

Oak Grove [2].4, *20*
oak trees [2].4, 10, 23; [9].7, 33; [10].6
   Queen Elizabeth's [1].*8*, *9*, 12
Oaklands [5].18; [9].39
Oakley, John, school [8].*30*, 31
oats [9].17, 20, 21, 47
Ochrens, Frederick Ferdinand [11].14
Odeon Cinema [12].13
Offley [6].14
Ofield, Miss (Headmistress) [8].32
oil miller [11].86
Old Coach House, Park Street [3].10; [10].*cover*, 19; [11].33
   OS grid ref. [10].32
Old Cottage, Bridge Road [10].17
   OS grid ref. [10].31
   plan [10].*14*

Old Fiddle Cottages [10].22
   OS grid ref. [10].32
   plan [10].*22*
Old Fiddle pub, Roe Green [2].*18*, 27; [3].*16*, 21, 31; [11].72
   sign [2].*26*
Old Hatfield [1].4; [11].3
Old Palace (Bishop's Palace; Great Stables; Morton's Palace; Tudor Palace) [1].4, 10, *13*, 16, 19; [2].10
   14c. [1].19
   rebuilt, *1480* [1].19; [10].7
   brickwork [7].7; [10].7; [11].66
   and church [7].7
   early manor house, timber [10].6, 7
   entrance gateway [1].*10*
   in *1603* [1].12
   1628 conversion [11].64
   OS grid ref. [10].32
   and school [8].8-9, 15, 20; [10].6
   stables [11].64
Old Parsonage (Old Rectory; Parsonage House) [1].*8*, 9, *13*, 17, *18*; [2].28; [7].9-12, *27*; [9].18 [10].10-11, *11*, 15; [11].53, 57, 63
   OS grid ref. [10].32
   plan [10].*9*, 10
   repaired, *1534* [7].10
   as school [8].4, 11, 31
Old School House [11].84
Old Vicarage [7].12
Old Workhouse Yard [11].*12*, 43
Oldings, Jack [5].7
Oldings Corner [1].*5*; [5].*32*
Oliver, B. H. [8].15, 32
Oliver, George [2].14
Oliver (alias Glover), Henry [11].38-9

Oliver, Lewis [2].13
Oliver, Sophia [11].26
Ollice, William [9].15
omnibus [11].88
One Bell inn [3].*8*, 14, 25, 26, 31; [5].30; [6].21; [11].6, *12*
O'Neill, Dr. [11].83
Onslow family [7].5, 10
   Onslow, Catherine [4].18
   Onslow, Edward [7].5
   Onslow, Sir Fulk [1].17-18; [4].18; [7].5, 10; [11].53
   Onslow, Richard [7].5, 10
Onslow School [1].18; [8].9, 15, 32
Open Field System [1].**12-14**, *13*, *14*; [9].9
open-plan design [10].30
orchid vans [5].19
organist [11].88
Orm, widow [11].19
Orme, Catherine Mary [11].34
Osbaldeston, Francis James [6].15; [11].10, 79
Osbaldeston, Dr. Lyttleton Frederick [11].10, 13, 83
Osbaldeston, Thomas [11].10, 13, 79, 83
Osbaldeston, Thomas junior [11].83
Osborn, Sir Frederick [12].4
Osborne, Peter [4].18
Osborne, Thomas, 1st Duke of Leeds [8].5, 8
ostlers [11].87
Our Lady Queen of Apostles Church [7].*20*, 31
Overseers of the Poor [6].11-12
Owsten, John [2].27
oxen [2].8; [9].19, 35
   tolls [1].11
Oxford Movement [7].21
Oxlease [1].4; [2].5; [7].27, 29; [9].16
Oxlease Drive [5].16; [7].27, 31
Oxleys pasture [2].5,*20*

P

Packer, Rev. G. [7].24
Packer, John [6].16
Packer, Sarah [6].17
Paddon, Dorcas [11].39
Paddon, Samuel [11].30, 39
Padget, T. L.
   author Part [8]
Page, Francis [6].13
Page, H. [8].12
Page, John [6].7
Page, Mr. (schoolmaster) [8].28
Page, Mrs. (of Union) [8].23
Page, Mrs. H. (schoolmistress) [8].12
Page's Mill [6].12
Pails family [2].30
Palace, Old *see* Old Palace
Pales family [11].54
Pallet, William [6].21
Palmer family [11].35-6, 52, 54, 71
   Palmer, Henry [11].36
   Palmer, John (lawyer, *18c.*) [11].79
   Palmer, John (wheelwright, *d.1785*) [11].*12*, 32, 35-6
   Palmer, John junior (*d.1796*) [11].36
   Palmer, John (*d.1811*) [11].35
   Palmer, Mary (née Lamb) [11].35
Palmerston, Henry John Temple, 3rd Viscount [2].32; [11].82; [12].5
Pankhurst, T. [2].14
pannage [1].16
Panshanger [1].*26*, 27
   estates [12].8
   farming [9].7, 29
pantry shops [12].12
paperhanger [11].86
paper-makers [11].*12*, 13, 22, 55, 61, **69-71**, 86
   union [6].**17**; [11].55

paper mills [5].13; [6].17, *18*;
   [9].*24*; [11].**69-71**
Papper, Thomas [2].14
Parish, Hatfield, *see* Hatfield Parish
Parish, John (priest) [2].12
Parish Church of St. Etheldreda
   [1].*cover*, 3, 24;
   [7].*cover*, 2, 6-9, *6*, *8*, *9*,
   16, 25, *27*, 30, 31
   attendance [6].24
   bells [7].7, 8; [11].67-8, *68*
   Brocket Chapel [7].7; [11].13
   chandelier [11].13
   chantries [7].7
   Chantry Chapel [2].8
   churchyard [11].81
      gates [7].9
   Communion plate [7].4, 8
   memorials [11].80
      Shallcross memorial [2].32
      Willis memorial [2].16
   Ponsbourne Aisle [4].13
   records [2].24
   restoration [8].5, 8-9, 26
   Salisbury Chapel [7].6-7, 8
   spire [7].8-9
   storm damage [12].25
   theft from [6].19
   yard [6].8
Parish Clerks [7].13; [8].31; [11].28,
   79
Parish Council [5].15
parish magazine, Hatfield
   1888 [7].16, 17-18
   1889 [8].23
   1893 [7].17
   1901 [7].14-15; [12].5
   files [12].6
Parish Rate [9].18
parish records [7].4; [11].4
parish registers [8].22; [11].3, 53, 75
parish schools [8].4
parish vestry [6].20
parishes [7].17, 19-20, 29
Park Grove [2].12

Park Street (Duck Lane) [3].*8*, 10,
   15; [5].6; [6].24;
   [11].*12*, 72
   bakers [11].33-5
   brewery [3].9
   butchers [11].31-3
   cottages sale [11].41, 43
   families [11]. 9, 22, 27, 62, 64,
      66, 71, 74, 85
   "Hill House" [11].84, *84*
   market [11].5
   Nos. 1-3 [10].15, 17, 20
      stairs [10].17, *18*
   Nos. 16-22 [11B]. *cover*
   No. 40 [11].7, 64
   OS grid ref. [10].32
   pubs [3].23, 29, 30, 32; [10].2,
      19
   school [8].30, 31
   trades [11].*28*, 31-6, 33
   viaduct [5].9; [11].7, 84
   wheelwrights [11].**35-6**
   20c. [12].12
Park Street Brewery [3].*8*
Park Street Chapel [7].23, [7].*23*,
   24-5, *27*, 30, 31;
   [10].28; [11].23, 39
Parkway [7].19
Parliament
   bounties paid [9].17
   Civil War [4].12
   Clerk [11].53
   Members [2].8; [4].11, 15
   and railway [5].9, 11, 12
Parnell, James [4].19
Parr, Anne [4].17-18
Parr, Catherine [4].11, 17
Parr, Mary Ann [8].26
Parr, William, Marquis of
   Northampton [4].17
Parrot, Thomas [11].14
Parrott family [11].54
   Parrott, Abraham [11].10
Parsonage *see* Old Parsonage

46

Parsonage Farm, North Mymms
    [2].*20*, 21; [9].18
Parsonage House *see* Old Parsonage
Parsons (clergy) [1].17, 24; [7].9,
    11; [11].78-9
    see also names
Partridge, Gabriel [3].29
pasture [1].16, 27; [9].10, 31, 32,
    44, 46
Patent Rolls [11].59
Payce, Reginald [6].16
Payne family [11].19, 43, 54
Peacock, Thomas [6].17
Pear Tree Farm [9].5, 3-2, 378
    beerhouse near [3].21, 32
Pear Tree pub [3].*16*, 21, 31
Pearman, James [6].19
Peartree [9].*24*, 30, 45; [11].61
    shops [12].12
Peasants' Revolt [1].20; [10].7
Peel, Sir Robert [6].22
Pegen, William [6].6
Pegeon, William [6].20
Pegeons [6].6
Pegram, William, school [8].*30*, 31
Peile, Rev. Benjamin [8].11, 31;
    [11].79
Pemberton, Goddard [7].5
Pembroke, earldom [4].8
Penn, Emily [8].27
Penrose, Francis [11].81
Penrose, James [11].*12*, 81
Pentecostal Church [7].*20*, 31
Pepper Alley (Hall) [2].**13-14**, *20*,
    25, 27; [9].9; [10].22
Pepys, Samuel [3].26, 28; [5].6-7;
    [7].7-8
Perry, Thomas [11].*12*
peruke makers [11].*12*, 25, 27
Pest House [9].16
Peterborough [5].*11*, 13, 14, 25
petrol station [4].22
Pettingell (railway employee)
    [11].40

Pettit, Joseph [6].15; [11].*12*, 27
Pettit & Co. [11].17-18
Petty France [11].36
Petty Sessional Court House [6].*26*,
    27, 28
Petty, William [4].23
Pevsner, Nikolas [3].14; [10].27
pewter [9].13
Phelps, Thomas [11].39
Philip de Eya [7].6
Phipp, Nathaniel [6].12
Phipps family [11].43
    Phipps, Mary [11].30
    Phipps, Nathaniel [11].24
    Phipps, William [11].6, 24
Pickett, William [6].19
Pickett's Farm House [7].16
Pickford Mill [11].70
Pigbornes Lane [1].21
pightlee [2].10, 16
Pigott's Directory [11].71
pigs [1].24, 29; [9].20, 27, 37, 40-1,
    44, 48
pig killer [11].86
Pikebon family [1].21
Pilkington, Hubert [4].16
pillory [6].7, *8*
pinder [6].7
Pinhorn, M.
    co-author Part [3]
Pinnock, Frances [11].34
Pittage field [1].*13*, 17, *18*, 24; [7].9
Place Farm [11].57
Plaistows [9].38
Platelayers Arms [3].*8*, 15, 18, 25,
    26, 31
Playle, W. H. [12].21
ploughboot [1].16
ploughing [9].*cover*, 19
ploughs [9].20, 22
Plowman, Hugh [1].22
plumbers [11].*12*, 14-15, 38, 86
    family pedigrees [11].42
plumbing [10].7

47

poaching [1].15; [6].19
Police
    Newgate Street [4].24
    origins [6].*cover*, 20-1
    radio [6].25-6
    Rural Police District [6].23
    see also County Police Force
Police Cottages [8].15
Police houses [7].25
Police Station [6].*23*, 25
Policewomen [6].27
pollution [7].15
Pond Field [2].21
Pond Hill [11].71
Pond Pightlee field strip [2].19
Ponsbourne (Ponsborne,
          Pumelesburne) [1].*15,
          20*; [4].7, **10-16**, 19, 22,
          26
    church [4].23-4; [7].21
    farms [9].6, 29, 32, 46
    map [4].*26*
    OS grid ref. [10].32
    school [8].31
Ponsbourne family [4].7-8
Ponsbourne House [4].*4, 5, 15*
Ponsbourne Manor [4].14-16; [10].9
    laboratory [4].25
Ponsbourne Manor Court [4].24
Ponsbourne Park [4].*4*, 6, 24-5;
    [7].30; [9].*25*
Ponsbourne Tunnel [4].*4*, 6, 25;
    [5].*17*
Ponsfall Farm [4].22; [9].46, 47
poor, the
    Act of Settlement [6].14-15
    bequest to [11].13
    education [8].10
    garments for [12].6
    poor relief [9].26
    poverty, *19c.* [9].26
    vagrancy [6].14-15
    see also Workhouse
Poor Law [6].11
Poor Law Commission [9].26

Poor Rate [9].19
poor relief [6].11-12; [9].26
Popes [9].*25*
Pope's Farm [2].19; [9].30, 32
Popes Manor [1].*13, 15, 20*; [4].*26*
    manor-house [10].9
    OS grid ref. [10].32
Poplars, the [3].31
population [5].4-5; [7].30; [8].30;
    [11].88; [12].11, 14, 20
post chaise [3].24
post chaise inn [3].12
Post Office [11].76-8; [12].22
postboys [11].87
Postern Gate [4].24
posting houses [3].9
Pot Kiln Field [9].27
Pot Kiln Lane [1].21
potash [6].13, 14
potatoes [9].20, 21, 27, 34, 35, 36,
    37, 38, 43, 47-8
    in diet [12].14
Poter, Bernard [1].19
Potter, Beatrix [12].6
Potter, Edward [10].12
Potter, Eliza [8].23
Potter, William [6].5
Potterells [9].38
potters [10].6, 7; [11].63
Potters Bar [7].28
    railway [5].12, 16, *17*, 19, 26,
        27
pottery [1].19; [10].6
Potwellgrove [6].6
poultry [9].12, 48
pounds (animal) [6].7
Powell family [11].43, 54
    Powell, Mark [11].22, 61, 70, 77
    school [8].*30*, 31
Poyner, Thomas [7].5
Pratchet, Charles [3].23
Pratchet, Mary Ann [3].23
Pratchett family [11].54, 62
    Pratchett, Caroline S., school
        [8].*30*, 31

Pratchett, Charles (farmer of Birchwood) [9].20, 21; [11].62
Pratchett, John [11].62
Pratchett, Leonard [3].23; [11].62
Pratchett, William [11].62
pre-fabs [10].30
Prentice, J. G. [8].31, 32
Presbytery [7].28-9
Preston, J. A.
 author Part [8]
Preyntys (alias Marten), Robert [11].24
Price family [11].53
prices [4].13-14; [6].5-6, 13
 barber's [11].29
 building materials [10].25
 carcasses [11].31
 farm produce [9].28
 inn charges [3].9
 between World Wars [12].13
 1963, table [12].*14*
Pricking-song (Prykking Song) [2].12; [6].4, [6].7
Priest, Rose [11].16
Primrose Cottages [8].15
Prince of Wales pub [3].15, 21, 23, 29
printers [5].19; [11].15
Priory House [3].23; [10].20-1, 28; [11].65, *65*, 73, 84
 OS grid ref. [10].23
 stairs [10].*18*
prison
 cage [6].7-8
 hulks [6].17
 lock-up [11].*12*
prisoners [6].16
Prisoners of War [4].26; [9].41
Pritchard, William [6].21
privies [6].6; [8].27
Privy Council [6].16
prize fighting [7].15
 professionals [11].**78-83**
 property ownership [6].8-9

Protectorate [6].20
Protestant Church [8].5
Protestant Dissenters [7].21-5
Pryor, Alfred [3].7
Pryor, Edward Vickris [3].7
Pryor, John [3].7
Pryor, Messrs. [3].15, 18
Pryor, Morris [3].7
Pryor, Reid & Co. [3].7, 8
Pryor Reid Brewery [11].74; [12].7
Public Library [8].*30*, 31
publicans [3].**23-6**; [9].30; [11].15, 42
pubs [3].4, 5, 6, *8*, **18-22**, 27
 see also ale-houses; inns; *names*
puddingstones [4].5, 6
pump [4].23
Punch [5].19, *20*
punishments
 legal [6].7-8, 17; [8].21; [11].5
 school [7].15; [8].23
Puttocks Oak
 pubs [3].13, 20, 29, 31
 school [8].11, 12, *30*, 31
Pye, Isaac [6].24
Pye, John [6].4
Pygges, Richard [6].7
Pym, Francis [5].27

Q

Quakers [3].7
Quarter Sessions [6].10, 13, 23-4, 28; [11].74, 79
 Records [4].24
Queen Elizabeth II hospital [12].15
Queensway [3].32; [7].17; [9].43; [11].*cover*
Queensway House [10].30; [12].5, 22
 OS grid ref. [10].23
Quickswood House [11].67
Quit Rent [2].16

R

Raban, Rev. Samuel [7].23

rabbits [1].15, 17; [6].19
racing [8].17; [11].61-2
Radcliffe, Sir Ralph [6].15
Ragmans farm [9].*25*
Railway Magazine [5].28
Railway Museum [5].25
railway stations [5].18, 19, 23
    Hatfield [1].4; [2].17, 31; [5].9,
        13, 15, 18, 21, 23;
        [11].78
    and mail [11].76-7, 78
    refreshment rooms [5].21
    WGC [5].16, 19, 20, *20*, 21;
        [12].*4*, 15
railways [1].6, *8*; [2].17; [5].**9-29**,
    17; [6].25; [9].16, 28,
    33, 38, 45; [11].40;
    [12].8
    accidents [5].4, 13, 27-9
    Act of Parliament, *1850* [5].9
    branch lines [4].6; [5].16-19
    bridges [1].4; [5].15, 16
    class [5].21
    employment [5].14
    first [5].9-12, [5].*10*
    first in Hatfield [5].5, 9
    and inns [3].12, 13, 18
    late *19c*. [5].21
    level crossings [1].10; [5].**15-16**
    loopline [5].26
    main line construction [5].12-13
    Newgate Street [4].*4*, 6, 24-5
    races [5].26
    Roe Green [2].31
    signals [5].28
    suburban [5].19-20
    timetable [5].22
    track widening [5].26
    tunnels *see separate entry*
    viaducts [5].9, *11*, 26, *27*
    in WWI [4].6
    in WWII [4].6
    see also Company names; trains
Raiment, Philip [11].6
Raiment, Sarah [11].6

Rainsford, Henry [7].11
Ralph de Blithe [4].10
Ramerick Manor [9].34
Randall, Charles [6].24
Randall, Charles Frank [11].42
Randall, Fanny [11].42
Randall, George [11].42
Randall, Isaac [11].42
Randall, James [11].12, 14
Randle, Ann [11].56
rat catchers [2].30; [11].64
Rates [9].30
    Poor Rate [9].19
Raven, Rev. [7].26
Rawley, John [11].25, 26
Rawley, Mary [11].26
Rawley, Thomas [11].25
Rawlins, John [7].21
Rawson, Luke (miller) [6].11;
    [7].11; [11].69
Ray, Rev. Thomas [11].25
    school [8].*30*, 31
Reading, Berkshire [5].18
Reading Rooms [12].6
Rectors [1].18; [7].2, 10-12; [9].26
    Cecil family as [7].12-15
    and schools [8].21-2, 26, 27, 28
    see also names: Abbot, Robert;
        Antrobus, Rev. Jocelyn
        James; Bagwell, Henry;
        Betts, William; Cecil,
        Rev. Charles; Eya,
        Philip de; Faithfull, Rev.
        Francis Joseph; Fuller,
        Rev. Thomas;
        Gascoyne-Cecil, Rev.
        Lord William; Grave,
        Rev. William Cecil;
        Keet, Rev. John (1752-
        1763); Keet, Rev. John
        (1788-1819); Lee, Dr.
        Richard; Leonard, Rev.
        Martin Patrick Grainge;
        May, William;
        Northwold, Nicholas;

Rainsford, Henry; Talbot, Rev. William Whitworth Chetwynd; Taylor, Rev. John; Wetheringsete, Robert
Rectory Drive school **[2]**.30; **[8]**.30, 31
Rectory Farm (Glebe) **[9]**.18, 21, *24*, 32, 46
Rectory (Parsonage House, Howe Dell) *see* Old Parsonage
Rectory (Vicarage), Fore Street **[7]**.10, 12; **[10]**.15; **[11]**.7, 11, *12*, 53, 77, 79, 80
  advowson **[7]**.7, 12
  OS grid ref. **[10]**.32
  plan **[10]**.*14*
  as school **[8]**.31; **[11]**.79
Red Lion Bridge **[8]**.16
Red Lion (old), Old London Road **[3]**.10-11, *16*, 31
Red Lion at Puttocks Oak **[1]**.10; **[3]**.13-14, *13*, 20, 24, 31; **[5]**.15; **[6]**.7, 21; **[9]**.*24*, 30, 33; **[10]**.28; **[11]**.6, *12*, 37, 61
  OS grid ref. **[10]**.32
Redbourn **[11]**.58
Reddall, Benjamin **[11]**.12
Reddell, Ralph **[6]**.14
Redhall Farm **[2]**.*20*, *28*
Reed Pond **[7]**.11
Reeves, James **[2]**.30
Reformation **[7]**.21, 28; **[8]**.4
refreshment rooms **[11]**.87
refrigerated ships **[9]**.42
refugees **[12]**.17
Rehabilitation Centre **[8]**.26
Reid, Lt. Geoffrey **[3]**.7
Reid, Percy Charles **[3]**.**[7]**.
Reid, R. H. **[4]**.5
Reiss, R. L. **[12]**.21
Renaissance **[8]**.4

rents **[1]**.17, 20; **[12]**.9
Repton, Humphrey **[1]**.15
Resting Seat Cottage **[2]**.25
Restoration **[4]**.12, 13; **[6]**.20-1; **[7]**.21; **[8]**.7
Reynolds, Mr. (photographer) **[5]**.25
Richard ad Collem **[2]**.24
Richard de Blancheville **[4]**.7
Richard the potter **[10]**.6
Richardson, Sir Albert **[3]**.13
Richardson, W. (builder, *fl. 1890*) **[7]**.18
Richardson, W. J. (builder, *fl. 1930*) **[11]**.66
Rickett Common **[3]**.21
Rickmansworth **[1]**.6
Riddell, Miss M. **[8]**.26
Riddle, Jasper **[2]**.27; **[11]**.43
Riddles estate **[2]**.*28*; **[11]**.31, 43,
Ridge Hill **[5]**.30
Ridgeway **[4]**.*4*
Riffin, William **[3]**.31
rights of common **[1]**.15-16; **[4]**.19; **[6]**.6
Rights of Way **[1]**.14; **[5]**.14; **[10]**.28; **[11]**.43, 78
  OS grid ref. **[10]**.32
riot
  1704 **[6]**.17
  1850 **[3]**.18
Rippin, Ambrose **[11]**.*12*
Rising Sun pub **[1]**.10, **[3]**.*16*, 20, 25, 31
Rivaz, Alexander Hugonin **[11]**.85
Rivaz, Elizabeth Ann **[11]**.85
River Colne **[1]**.25, 27; **[12]**.25
River Lea **[1]**.4, 11, 17, *25*, 26, 27; **[4]**.*26*; **[5]**.6, 7, 27; **[9]**.31; **[11]**.69, 70; **[12]**.8
  Broadwater **[1]**.12
  diverted **[9]**.23
River Mimram **[5]**.11-12
road accidents **[5]**.29; **[8]**.25

51

road signs [5].*cover*, 29, *29*
roads [1].**4**, *5*, **8-11**, 13, 16, 25-6;
  [2].14; [5].**5-9**; [9].45,
  46
  Roman [1].25-6, *25*; [4].21;
    [5].5
  in *19c.* [7].14
  in *20c.* [5].29-30
  maintenance / surfacing [4].24;
    [5].8, 29; [6].12, 13;
    [9].16
  names [2].**32**
  Turnpike Road [2].*18*; [9].16
  see also tolls; *roadnames*
Robards, Sarah [11].56
robbery [11].64
Robert (Norman soldier) [1].23
Robert atte Delle [2].24
Robert de Kendall [6].10
Robert de Ponsbourne [4].7, 8
Robertson, Archibald, Chief
  Constable [6].22
Robin Hood pub [3].*17*, 21, *22*, 25,
  31; [5].13
Robins Way [12].*24*
Robinson, Rev. Charles James
  [7].16; [8].26, 27
Robinson, Mrs. Charles James
  [8].23, 26
Robinson, Thomas (post-boy,
  c.1761) [11].76
Roche Products [12].15
Rochester [7].5
Roe (Row, Rowe) **Green** [1].*6*, 22,
  24; [2].*cover*, **4-32**, *28*;
  [12].6
  early development [2].**25-9**
  1777 [2].*28*
  later development [2].**31**
  in *1851* [2].25, **29-31**
  1908 [2].*29*
  1949-50s [2].*22*; [12].22, 26
  modern street plan [2].*6*
  ash tree [2].23
  boundaries [2].4, *7*, 23

church [7].29
cottages [10].22
families [2].24-5; [11].43, 61,
  72
farms [9].6, 7, 9, 10, 33, 43, 46
housing [2].31
name [2].4
North [9].*24*, 44, 46
South [9].*24*, 30, 46
Roe Green Farm [2].17; [11].34
  1851 [2].30
  bungalows [2].31
Roe Green Farm North [2].*6*, 7, 13,
  15-16, *15*
Roe Green Farm South (South
  Farm) [2].*6*, 7, 13, 17,
  19, *20*; [10].12
  OS grid ref. [10].32
Roe Green Homestead [2].13
Roe Green Lane [1].22, 25; [1].4, *6*,
  7, *18*, *20*, 32; [3].21-2,
  31; [9].29
  1949 [2].*23*
  name [1].32
  pub [3].21-2, 31
  Toll Gate [2].27
Roe Green Mission Room [7].17-
  18, *27*, 31
Roe Hill House [2].31; [7].*27*;
  [11].40
Roe Hyde (Roe Hide) [2].*6*, *20*, 24;
  [6].18-19
Roe Hyde Common [2].17
Roe Hyde Farm [2].5, 9, 12, 13, **14**,
  17; [9].44, 46
Roe Stock [2].21
Roebuck (Nag's Head) alehouse,
  Fore Street [3].30;
  [11].6, *12*, 24
Roebuck Farm [9].44
Roebuck inn, Lemsford [3].13, *16*,
  31; [9].30
Roger de Louth [2].8; [6].10
Roger de Luda [4].16
Roger of Essendon [1].20-1

52

Roger, Thomas [6].19
Rogers, John [6].19; [7].7
Rolfe, Agnes [3].5; [6].6
Roman Catholic Church [7].27-30
Roman Catholic priests *see*
　　　Arbuthnott, Fr. David;
　　　Brown, Monsignor
　　　Henry Barton; Milne,
　　　Fr.; Vaughan, Dr.
　　　Herbert; Vaughan, Fr.
　　　Kenelm; Williams, Fr.
　　　Percy Hemus
Roman Empire [8].4
Roman Roads [1].**25-6**, *25*; [4].21;
　　　[5].5
Roman Way [2].*28*
roofs [10].5, 7, 8
Rookwood, Dorothy [11].10
Rose and Crown alehouse, Fore
　　　Street (*1605*) [3].*17*, 31;
　　　[11].27
Rose and Crown, Tyler's Causeway
　　　[3]. *17*, 31; [4].23
Rose and Crown pub, Wellfield
　　　Road [3].*17*, 21, 31
Rosedale Cottages [2].31
Ross, Charles [11].10
Ross, Mary [11].10, 37-8
Rothehyde, Aleyn de la [2].14, 17,
　　　24
Round-London Railway [5].18
Row (pub owner) [3].29
Rowe *see* Roe
Royal College of Physicians [11].79
Royal College of Surgeons [11].79
Royal Mail [11].76
Royal Oak inn [3].30
Royal Show [9].44
Royal visitors [8].18
　　　Edward VII [12].6, 7
　　　Victoria [7].8; [8].18; [12].26
Royston [5].5, 7
Rucks Farm [4].20
Rudge, Dr. [4].5

Rumania [9].41
Rumbold, Audrey [4].18
Rumbold, John [4].18
Rumney family [11].62
Rural District [7].29; [12].11
Rural District Council [3].26;
　　　[11].46, 60, 76, 78;
　　　[12].9, 20
Rural Library [12].6
Rural Police District [6].23
Russell, Lavinia [3].26
Russell family [3].26
Ryde, The [9].30
　　　celebratory bonfire [12].7
　　　Cockaigne Housing Group
　　　[12].11
Ryder, William [6].24
Ryder's Seed Trial Ground [2].5, 14

S

Sacriston, Adam [1].22
saddlers [11].11, *12*, 19, 27, 86
Saffron Close (Malting Mead)
　　　[11].38
salesmen [11].86
Salisbury Arms (White Lion / Lyon)
　　　inn [1].10; [3].*8*, *11*, 11-
　　　12, 24, 27, 31; [5].13;
　　　[7].13; [8].10; [11].6, 7,
　　　12, 24, 40, 76, 77;
　　　[12].13
Salisbury Arms Tap [3].30;
　　　[11].*cover*
Salisbury estate [9].16
Salisbury family [5].13; [7].6;
　　　[12].8
　　　property owned by [11].*8*
　　　see also Cecil family; *titles*
Salisbury, Robert Cecil, 1st Earl
　　　of [1].11-12, *14*, 15, 17;
　　　[9].9
　　　and enclosure [1].14, 16; [4].21,
　　　22
　　　furniture inventory [10].10

acquires Hatfield Park and
    builds Hatfield House
    [1].11-12; [9].7; [10].7
Home (Lawn) Farm [1].8, 9, 10,
    17
imprint [10].7
provision for Poor [6].11
and rectory advowson [7].5-6,
    11
Salisbury, William Cecil, 2nd Earl
    of [11].5, 63, 64, 69, 73,
    79
Pepys observes [7].7
Salisbury, James Cecil, 3rd Earl
    of [2].13
Salisbury, James Cecil, 4th Earl of
    [11].5-6, 69
Salisbury, James Cecil, 5th Earl of
    [4].13; [7].12; [8].6
Salisbury, Lady Anne Tufton, 5th
    Countess of [8].6
endows school [5].13; [8].5, 6-7
Salisbury, James Cecil, 6th Earl of
    childhood [8].6
    family [7].12, 13
    landlord [9].23; [11].7
    and school [8].5
Salisbury, James Cecil, 1st
    Marquess of [7].13;
    [11].7, 24, 25, 27, 35,
    38, 40, 54, 67, 81
schoolboy [8].31
home farm [9].18
inns owned by [3].9, 10-11, 12,
    30, 31
Salisbury, Lady Emily Mary Hill,
    1st Marchioness of
farming [9].19, 20, 21, 22
presentation to church [7].8
death [3].27; [11].82
Salisbury, James Gascoyne-Cecil,
    2nd Marquess of [2].11;
    [5].13; [6].19; [7].13;
    [8].31; [11].82
and churches [7].8, 15, 16

farming [9].26, 29, 30, 33
and Hatfield House [7].9
and London Road School [8].11
and Militia [8].17
and paper-mill lease [11].70
and Police [6].22, 23-4
and pubs [3].29, 30
and railway [1].8; [5].9, 12, 15-
    16
and road surfacing [5].8
Salisbury, Robert Cecil, 3rd
    Marquess of [8].17;
    [11].19
builds churches [7].12, 16
builds cottages [10].24, 29
education [8].4
and farms [9].5, 37-8, 40, 45
and Golden Jubilee [8].18
and housing [9].43; [12].5
and railway [5].21, 23, 25
and school [7].14; [8].8
and St. Luke's [7].17
statue [1].4
and viaduct [11].7
Salisbury, Georgina Alderson, 3rd
    Marchioness of
and Church schools [7].18;
    [12].5-6
Salisbury, James Edward Hubert
    Gascoyne-Cecil, 4th
    Marquess of [7].25;
    [12].6
cars [7].13
as child [7].8
9th birthday [8].24
and schools [8].12-13, 15
(as Viscount Cranborne) and Boer
    War [12].7
sells land for Garden City [12].8
and Hatfield New Town Plan
    [12].19
Salisbury, Lady Cicely Alice
    Gore, 4th Marchioness
    of [2].31; [8].18
and schools [8].9, 15

54

Salisbury, Robert Cecil, 5th
    Marquess of
  allows access to archives [1].3;
    [2].3; [3].3; [5].3; [8].3;
    [10].3; [11].3, 52
  and Cavendish Hall [7].18
  and Countess Anne School [8].9
  farms [9].46
  and Rectory [7].12
Salisbury Hall [12].17
Salisbury Hotel [3].*8*, 14, 31; [8].31;
    [10].28; [11].78
"Salisbury Line" [12].20
Salisbury Square [7].7; [8].17;
    [11].43
Salter, M. (of Millward's) [10].6
Salvation Army
  Hatfield [7].27, 31
  W.G. C. [7].*20*, 31
Salver, Richard [3].5; [4].23
Sambrook, Jeremy [3].30
Sambrook, Judith [3].30
Sammell, John [9].16
sampler [8].6
Sams, William [11].43, 44
sanatorium [2].31
sand [1].26, 27; [2].20
Sanders, Dame Agnes [1].*cover*
Sanders, Messrs. [5].19
Sandridge [9].41
Sandy Croft [2].*20*, 21
Sandys, Duncan [12].22
Saumarez, Martha [11].85
Saunders family [2].24
  Saunders, Alice Jeannette [11].85
  Saunders, John [11].43
  Saunders, William [9].10
Savage, Fr. Stanislaus [7].29
Savill, Mrs. (of Post Office) [11].78
sawmills [9].33
Sawyer, B. Robinson [4].22
Saxons [1].*25*; [6].5
Say family chart [4].*17*
Say, Henry, Earl of Essex [4].17
Say, Sir John [4].17

Say, Sir William [4].17
Saye, Arthur W. [11].22
scale makers [11].86
Scarborough family [3].30
Scarborough, Joseph [5].9
Scarborough, Percy Charles
    [11].26
Scare, John [11].67
School Boards [8].20
school camp [4].*4*, 5; [9].7
School House [8].10-11; [11].67
School Lane [1].10; [5].15; [8].9,
    13, 32
School of Music and Drama [8].32
school Treats [8].24
schoolmasters [11].79, 88
school mistresses [2].30; [7].15;
    [8].5, 9, 10, 12, 27, 29,
    32
schools [8].3-32, *30*
    19c.[7].15
    1850/1 [2].30; [5].13
  age of admittance [8].6, 29
  Batterdale [3].30
  boarding [4].5; [11].25
  Board Schools [8].20
  chronology [8].31-2
  County Council [8].15, *30*, 32
  elementary [8].10
  fees [8].23
  Fore Street [8].5, 10, 11, 31, 32;
    [11].25
  Inspectors [8].8, 20, 26-9
  Log Books [8].16-26
  Newgate Street [4].*4*, 16, 20, 24
  registers [8].6, *16-17*, 28
  Roman [8].4
  Roman Catholic [7].29-30
  since *1930* [8].30
  voluntary societies [8].10
  see also Church of England
    Schools; National
    Schools; Sunday
    Schools; *names of*
    schools

Scottish farmers
  9c. [9].34-6, 43
  20c. [9].44-5
S. E. & C. Railway [5].26
Sear, Marcella [11].16
Searancke family [3].6, 9, 14, 19,
  23, 29, 30, 31, 32;
  [11].8, 9-11, 24, 27, 29,
  31, 35, 38, 63, 84
  descendants (table) [11].10
Searancke, Dionise [11].59
Searancke, Elizabeth [11].10
Searancke, F. C. [11].12
Searancke, Francis Carter [3].6-7
Searancke, Grace [11].83
Searancke, James [11].10
Searancke, John [3].19; [9].13, 18;
  [11].9, 10, 11, 13, 24,
  31, 37, 66-7
Searancke (later Hare), Mary
  [11].36-7
Searancke, Sarah [11].10
Searancke, Thomas (fl. 1619)
  autograph [3].6
Searancke, Thomas (b.1620)
  [11].10
Searancke, Rev. Thomas of
  Chevely, Cambs. (b
  1652) [11].10, 11
Searancke, Rev. Thomas (fl.
  1716) [3].14
Searanke's Brewery [11].9, 11, 36,
  58
Searle, Mrs (schoolmistress) [8].27
Seaton, Rev. D. [8].21
Seaton, E. W. [4].3
secretaries [11].88
Sellwood, Richard [6].13
Sellwood, William [6].14
Selwyn housing estate [2].4, 17
Sequeira, M. [4].3
servants [9].15
Service, Janet [2].11
Service, John [2].11; [9].34
settlement [6].14-15

Seven Stars inn see Bull inn
sexton [11].27, 80
Sexton family [4].16
  Sexton, R. L. F. [8].32
Seymour, George [11].27
Seymour, Jane [4].17
Seymour, Sir Thomas [4].11, 17
Seymour Clarke, Mrs. [8].24
Shallcross Crescent [2].32
Shallcross, Julia [2].32
Shand, Simon [11].67
Sharp, A. E. [11].22
Sharpe, Menzies [4].16
Sharpesbrach Common Field [2].14,
  17
Sharples, Charles [11].28
Shaw, James (priest) [2].8
Shaw, John (fl. 1607) [10].9, 10
Shawe, Richard [6].16
Sheehan, John, school [8].30, 31
Sheehan, Lavinia, school [8].30, 31
Sheehan-Dare, Caroline, school
  [8].30, 32
Sheehan-Dare, J. R. [8].31, 32
sheep [1].24; [2].17; [6].11; [9].12,
  17, 27, 42, 44
  buying [9].14, 17
  diseased [9].34
  pens [9].17
  prices [11].29, 31
  rearing [9].13, 23
  stealing [6].22, 23
  stray [6].7
  tolls [1].11
Sheldon, Edward [4].12
shepherds [11].86
Sheppard, Mary (née Dunn) [11].10,
  13
Sheppard, Richard [11].10
Sheriffs (officers) [2].8; [6].10
Sherrards Park wood [1].4
Sherrards Wood [12].8, 9
Sherrardswood School [12].24
Sherrell, Rev. [7].24
Sherriff family [9].3, 40-1

Sherriff, A. J. (of Nashes Farm) [9].41
Sherriff, Arthur James (*fl. 1872*) [3].7, 9; [9].40, 41, 43; [11].62
Sherriff, Eric [9].41
Sherriff, G. L. [9].3, 41, 46
Sherriff, Leslie [9].41
Sherriff, Mr. (*fl. 1900*) [9].34
Sherriff (née Crawford), Mrs. [9].41
Sherriff's Brewery [3].8-9
Shiers, Sir George [4].19
Shiers, Robert [4].19
Shillito, H. T. (architect) [7].17, 18; [10].24
shingle-layer [10].6
shingles [10].6
shoemakers [11].19-20, 27, 86
   inventory [11].20-1
shoe warehouse [11].87
shooting [6].20; [9].30
shopkeepers [11].*12*, 67, 87
   table [11].34
   see also trades
Shoplands [12].22
shops
   Fore Street [11].11-15, *17*, 17-27, 28-9
   inventories
     1724, of collar-maker [11].18-19
     1726, of shoe-maker and Woman's shop [11].19-21
     1869, of Tingey's [11].44-5
   Newgate Street [4].24
   Park Street [11].27-8, 31-40, 44-6, *44, 45*
   WGC [12].11-12, 13
   20c. [12].11-13, 22
Shortridge, Hugh [4].19
Show Field [9].40; [11].*12*
Shredded Wheat Factory [12].*cover*, 15

Sibley family [11].62
Sigrave, Esther [11].26
silk mill [5].13
Silkin, Lewis [12].19
Silten House [3].18; [7].28, 31
Silver Jubilee train [5].27, *27*
Simkins, Edmund [11].*12*, 14
Simkins, James [11].14, 61
Simmons, Ann [11].42
Simmons, Arthur William [11].42
Simmons Cake Shop [2].25
Simmons, Charles [2].25; [11].42
Simmons, R. (Caterers) [3].31
Simmons, Reginald Charles [11].26, 42, 44
Simonshide [7].18
Simpkins, Edmund [11].61
Sinclair, Mr. (of Essendonbury) [9].32
Sinclair (of Harpsfield) [2].12
Sinclair, George [9].3, 37
Sinclair, James [9].35-8, 45
Sinclair, R. [9].3, *35*
Sisters of Mercy [7].29
Skegg, Sarah [11].30
Skeggs, William [8].25
Skillman, William [11].26, 27
Skinner's Company [8].4
Skips Grove [2].4, *20*
Skipsey, Benjamin [11].*12*
slate [10].7
slaughter house [11].14, 29
Slaughter, Mary [4].13
Slaughter, Paris [4].13
Sleapshyde [7].26
Slight family [3].23
Slough [5].18
Slow, Henry and Thomas [6].12
Smallford [3].26; [5].18; [11].58
small holdings [9].4, 5, 6, 7, 12, 23, 32, 46, 47
smallpox [5].13; [8].19; [9].16; [11].82
Smart, Josiah [11].66

Smith family (of Fore Street) [11].19
Smith family (of Roe Green) [2].24-5; [11].52
Smith, Francis [6].17
Smith, Henry [6].13
Smith, Hugh [7].21
Smith, John (baker) [11].22, 27, 32, 34
Smith, John [2].10 (farmer, c.*1650*)
Smith, John [6].18 (farmer, c.*1826*)
Smith, L. B. (petrol station owner) [4].22
Smith, Lydia [11].34
Smith, Martha [11].30
Smith, Mary [11].30
Smith, Mary Ann [11].34
Smith, Mr. (farmer, c.*1851*) [2].30
Smith, Sam [2].25
Smith, Susanna [11].10
Smith, Thomas [11].37-8
 school [8].*30*, 31
Smith, William [2].30
Smithfield [1].11; [9].44
 Cattle Market [9].33
smiths [11].71, 72, 87
 blacksmiths [4].5, 22; [11].*12*, 73-4
 Goldsmith [11].54-5
 shoeing smiths [11].87
 whitesmith [11].67
Smith Square [2].25
Smith, Walter the [2].11, 24-5
smoke chamber [10].11
smoking [5].13
Smollett, Tobias [3].26, 28
Society of Friends [7].*20*, 31
soil [9].4, 27
 sub-soil [1].*26*
soldiers [7].15
Somerset House [9].10
song-book [6].4, 7
Sorrel [2].19-*20*

Sorrel Sauce Field [2].16, *20*
Sothwell, Francis [7].7
South Down Road [2].11
South Field [2].17, *18*
Southgate [5].19
Southampton [8].5, 7, 8
South Herts Grass Belt [9].46
Southwode, John [2].20
Soyer, Alexis [12].6
Spalding and Myers [7].25
Sparrow, John [2].16
speculatists [11].41
Speaight, F. W. [10].27; [11].25, 66
Speaight, Mr. (Business Manager) [8].15
Spencer, Sir John [6].14
spickets [11].21
Spring arable field strip [2].19
Spring Glen [2].32
Spring Villas [11].39
Spurgeon, Mr. (*fl. 1862*) [7].24
Spurling, Bartholomew [11].14, 80
Spurrell, James [3].7
Squire, Thomas [11].6
Squires, George [9].12
St. Albans [4].19; [7].11; [11].79; [12].19
 Abbot [7].10
 Beasney family [11].28-9
 boundary [2].4, 23
 buses [5].30
 Cemetery [7].28
 Gape family [2].12; [9].34
 market [9].36
 Marlborough Almshouses [11].68
 Police [6].27
 post [11].77
 railway [5].15-16, 18-19, 22, 23
 Searanke family [11].11
 See [7].5
 Vale of [9].47
 Winderich Manor [4].10
 see also St. Peter's Parish
St. Albans Abbey [7].5; [11].57

St. Albans Co-operative Society
    [12].11
St. Albans Road [1].7, 10, 14;
    [2].17; [3].29, 30, 31,
    32; [5].15; [7].28;
    [8].32; [9].29; [11].78;
    [12].13-14, 15
  Flint cottages [10].7, 8, 28
  OS grid ref. [10].31
St. Anne's Chantry [2].8, 12
St. Audrey's
    built, *1888* [7].12
  Blind Home [3].19, 32; [7].12
St. Audrey's School [2].5; [7].25;
    [8].12, *13*, 14-15, 25,
    14, 29, 32
St. Bonaventure church [7].*20*, 31
St. Charles house [7].28
St. Dominic's Priory [4].16
St. Etheldreda's Church *see* Parish
    Church of St. Etheldreda
St. Francis of Assisi church [7].*20*,
    31
St. James's Review, The [11].18, 22,
    47, 72
St. James Tile Company [4].25
St. John's church, Hilltop [1].*cover*;
    [3].22; [7]. 17-19, *27*,
    30, 31; [12].22
St. John's church, Lemsford [7].16,
    20, 21, 31
St. John's House [7].18
St. Luke's cemetery [12].17
St. Luke's church [7].17, 18, 21, *27*,
    30, 31
St. Mark's church [7].15, 16, 21, 31
St. Mary Magdalene's church
    [7].16-17, 19, *20*, 31
St. Mary the Virgin chapel [7].15
St. Mary's, Ponsbourne [4].*cover*,
    24; [7].21, 31
St. Mary's School [8].*30*, 31
St. Michael and All Angels church,
    Birchwood [7].*20, 27*,
    30, 31

St. Michael and All Angels church,
    Ludwick [7].*20*, 31
St. Michael's house [1].9; [3].30;
    [11].63
St. Michael's Manor [2].12
St. Neots [3].12; [5].11
St. Peter's Church [7].*27*, 31
St. Peter's Cottages [10].*23*, 24;
    [12].5
  OS grid ref. [10].32
St. Peter's Parish, St. Albans [2].4,
    7, 12, 16, *20*; [3].21;
    [6].18; [7].29
St. Peter's Tithe Map [2].17
St. Raphael's Colony [7].30
St. Theresa's parish [7].29, 30, 31
stage coaches [3].9
Staines family [11].43, 54
Staines, Eliza [11].56
Staines, Elsie [8].2
Staines (railway employee)
    [11].40
stairs [10].15, 17, *18*, 20, 21
Stamford [3].24
Stanborough (Stanborrowe,
    Standborough) [5].9;
    [6].11; [11].59
  Bull inn [3].13, *16*, 24, 29;
    [9].30; [11].59
  church [7].22
  cottages [10].22
  farms [9].6, 7, 10, *24*, 30, 46
  OS grid ref. [10].32
  plan [10].*22*
Stanborough Bury
    (Stanboroughbury)
    [1].16; [9].40, 48
Stanborough corner [1].11
Stanborough Farm [9].14-16, 18,
    14, 32, 41, 42, 46;
    [10].17, 19; [11].61
  OS grid ref. [10].32
Stanborough hill [1].26
Stanborough House [10].28
  OS grid ref. [10].32

Stanford, H. E. **[8]**.32
Stanmore **[7]**.11
Stansted Abbots **[3]**.7
Starkey Engineering Company
   [11].71
Starkey family **[11]**.62
   Starkey, James **[11]**.71
   Starkey, Joseph **[11]**.71
   Starkey, Thomas **[11]**.71
Starr, Elizabeth **[11]**.56
stationers **[11]**.22, 23, 87
stations *see* railway stations
Steabben family **[11]**.29
Steamer inn **[3]**.*16*, 31
Stephenson (bailiff) **[9]**.22
Stephenson, George **[5]**.11
Stevenage **[5]**.7
   Hundred Court **[6]**.10
   new town **[12]**.19, 21
   Pepys in **[5]**.6
   railway **[5]**.12, 21, 26
Stevens, Samuel **[7]**.11
stewards **[11]**.88
Stewart, Halley **[7]**.25
Stirling, Miss (Headmistress) **[8]**.32
Stock (Stoke) Hide (Hyde)
   (Stockhide, Stokehyde)
   [1].*20*, 21; **[2]**.4, 5, 8, 9,
   11, 13, *20*; **[4]**.*26*; **[6]**.9;
   [9].5
stock (farm animals) **[9]**.43-4
Stockbreach **[9]**.*24*
Stockbreach Common **[1]**.*14*, 14;
   [11].43
Stockbreach Common Field **[2]**.12,
   15, 16, 17, *20*; **[9]**.*29*
Stockbreach Road **[1]**.7
stocks (punishment) **[6]**.7, 8, *9*
stockings **[11]**.20. 21
Stocks, Frederick **[11]**.27
Stocks, Thomas **[11]**.27
Stockton **[5]**.9
Stoke family **[2]**.8
   Stoke, John **[9]**.5
Stone, Elizabeth **[11]**.34

Stone, James Dunton **[11]**.34, 35
Stone, Lawrence **[10]**.8
Stone, Mr. (Roe Green farmer)
   [9].33
Stone House (Stonehouse; Clock
   House) Hotel **[1]**.4, *5*;
   [3].14, *16*, 31; **[5]**.*32*;
   [7].*27*; **[12]**.*13*, 13
Stonecross **[11]**.37
Stonecross Common **[1]**.*14*
Stonecross field **[9]**.9, 13
Stonecross Mead **[2]**.16
Stonecross Road **[1]**.7; **[7]**.25
Stonehills **[12]**.12
Stoney Field **[2]**.16
Storage (farm houses) **[10]**.15
stores *see* shops
storms **[12]**.24-5
Strathbogie family **[4]**.8-10
   Strathbogie, David, 11th Earl of
      Atholl **[4]**.9
   Strathbogie, David, 12th Earl of
      Atholl **[4]**.9
   Strathbogie, David, 13th Earl of
      Atholl **[4]**.9, 10
   chart **[4]**.*9*
straw **[9]**.18, 19, 21, 36
   burning **[6]**.13, 14
   plaiting **[2]**.30; **[9]**.23
straw dealers **[11]**.86
straw hats **[2]**.30; **[5]**.18, 19; **[8]**.23
Strawberry Field **[2]**.16, *20*
Streader family **[11]**.43, 54
   Streader, Ernest **[11]**.42
   Streader, James **[11]**.42
   Streader, Joseph **[11]**.42
   Streader, Thomas William
      [11].42, 46
   Streader, William **[11]**.42
streets **[4]**.6
   names **[2]**.32
   see also street names
Stride (farmer) **[9]**.44
Strode family **[4]**.14
   Strode, Samuel **[4]**.13

Stroud, Dorcas [11].30
Stroud, Lydia (*d.1799*) [11].30, 31, 33, 35
Stroud, Samuel [11].*12*, 31, 30, 33
Stuart, Lady Arabella [4].18
sub-manors [1].*20*, 23, 24; [10].9
Succession Duty [9].30
Suffel, William [4].7
sugar [12].14
sugar beet [9].48
Sullivan, Lawrence [4].14
Sun Insurance Office [3].14
Sun pub [3].*16*, 20, 24, 31
Sunday Savings Club [9].26
Sunday Schools [7].18, 23; [8].21-2, 24
surgeons [11].10, *12*, 13, 14, 25, 79-83, 88
surnames [1].20, 21-2
Surveyor of Highways [6].12
surveyors [5].8; [11].88
surveys
   13c. [5].4
   1607 [9].9-10
   land [9].19, 46-8
   Ordnance Survey map, *1961* [11].2, *op.* 49; 12 *op.* 1
Sutton, Rev. Peter [7].18
Suttons Farm [2].13; [9].*24*, 29, 32, 44, 46, 48
"Swan" house [7].10
Swan inn (Stevenage) [3].24
Sycamore Avenue [7].29
Symon [1].21
Symondshide (Symondshyde) [1].*6*, *20*, 21, 22, 23; [2].14; [4].9, *26*
   court rolls [6].5
   farms [9].5, 6, 18, 20, 21, 22, *24*, 29, 30, 32, 44, 46, 48
   tithes [7].10
   Wood [9].7, *24*, 33
Symondshide manor-house [10].9-10

OS grid ref. [10].32
Symondshyde Farm [11].60
Symondshyde Wood [9].7, *24*, 33
Symon-son-of-Adam [1].22
Synagogue [7].*20*, 31

T

tailors [11].*12*, 26, 27, 28, *28*, 43, 87
Talbot, Clare [11].3, 52
Talbot, Mrs. William Whitworth Chetwynd [8].22
Talbot, Rev. William Whitworth Chetwynd [7].13; [8].21-2, 26, 27, 28
tallage [2].8
Tan Yard [11].31
Tankard (publican) [3].24
tanks [8].25; [12].7
tanners [11].*12*, 38-40, 87
tasker [11].86
Tasker (later Walby), Martha [11].30, 31-2, 35
Tate, John [11].69
Tattorn, William [4].17
Tavener, Miss [8].23
taverns [3].4, 15
taxation [9].30
Tayler, Thomas [11].14
Tayler, William [11].14
Taylor family [2].11
   Taylor, Mr. (of Down's Farm) [2].11
   Taylor, Emmeline Agnes [11].26
   Taylor, George [8].23
   Taylor, John (poet) [3].2
   Taylor, Rev. John [7].10
   Taylor, Robert, J.P. [4].20, 24
   Taylor, Robert (Dissenter) [7].22
Taylor, Walker & Co. [3].29, 31
tea
   in *19c.* [7].14
   in *20c.* diet [12].14
   Mazawattee [11].18

61

Technical College [1].*5*; [2].11, 12-13; [5].*32*; [8].32; [9].46, 48; 106; [12].26
OS grid ref. [10].31
Telford (surveyor) [5].8
Temple Bar [11].75, 76
Templewicombe [4].11
Terry, Garnet [4].19-20
Tharp family [9].30. 41; [11].7, 16, 59
  Tharp, Ann [11].16, 59
  Tharp, Hannah [11].28
  Tharp, Joseph [11].16, 28
  Tharp, Sarah (*d.1730*) [11].16, 59
  Tharp, Sarah (*d.1794*) [11].16, 59
  Tharp, Sarah (*d.1828*) [11].16, 59
  Tharp, Sarah (née Eversall) [11].16
  Tharp, Sarah (née Johnson) [11].15, 16
  Tharp, William (of Stanborough, *d.1730*) [3].29; [11].16, 59
  Tharp, William (of Handside, *d.1762*) [11].16, 59
  Tharp, William (*d.1786*) [11].16, 59
Thatcher, James [3].9
theft (burglary, larceny) [6].7, 17, 18, 19, 21, 22
Theobalds [1].11; [9].9
Thistley Field [2].*20*
Thomas family [11].62
  Thomas, Conrad [11].34
  Thomas, Eliza [11].34
  Thomas, Frank [11].34
  Thomas, James Dunton [11].34
  Thomas, Jim [11].77
  Thomas, John [11].22, 34
  Thomas, Minnie [11].34
  Thomas, Miss (schoolmistress) [8].*30*, 32
  Thomas, Rebecca [11].34
  Thomas, Ruth [8].23; [11].34
  Thomas, Thomas [11].34
  Thomas, Dr. William Lloyd [11].82
  Thomas, William (wheelwright) [11].34
Thomas de la Haye [6].10
Thompson, Anne [6].14
Thorpe, Jacob [11].34
Thrale, Sarah [3].14
Three Roods at the Gate field strip [2].19
Thrift Club [12].6
Tidder *see* Tydder
Tiger Moth aircraft [11].50, *cover*
tiles [1].19; [4].25; [10].6-7; [11].63
  asbestos [10].8
  price [10].25
timber [1].19, 24; [2].10, 19, 23; [9].7, 30, 33; [10].5-6; [11].24, 69, 72
  licensing [6].14
  price [10].25
timber frame [10].5, 10, 12
Times, The [5].14
Tims, Geoffrey [3].31
Tims, R. J. [3].31
Tingey family [11].62
  Tingey, Arabella [11].42
  Tingey, Edmund Thomas [7].17; [11].42, *44*, 46
  Tingey, Emily Persa (née Randall) [11].42
  Tingey, Eric (furnisher) [11].42
  Tingey, John (bricklayer, *b.1802*) [11].42
  Tingey, John (baker, *b.1834*) [11].42, 44, 45
  Tingey, John (grocer, *b.1878*) [11].42, *44*, 46
  Tingey, Jonathan Edmund (grocer, *b 1843*) [11].42, 44-5, *44*, 78
  Tingey, Mary Ann [11].42
  Tingey, Norman William [11].42
  Tingey, Randall John [11].42
  Tingey, Rex Edmund [11].42

Tingey's (Corner) shop [11].46;
    [12].12
Tipping, Warrand [4].23
tippling house [3].5; [6].6
Tithe Award plans [9].28
Tithe Farm Map, *1824* [2].19
Tithe Map, *1838* [8].10-11; [9].28-31
Tithe-barns [7].11
Tithes [7].10, 11; [9].18
tithings [6].5
Todwell Field [1].*13*
Tokeley, Robert [4].12
Toleration Act [7].21
Toll Gate Farm [9].*35*
toll gates [1].11; [2].*18*, 27
toll-houses [1].11; [5].7, *8*
tolls [1].11; [5].8; [11].73
Tolmers [4].*4*, 5, 7, **16-20**, *20*, *26*; [9].6, *25*
Tolmers Hospital [4].25
Tolmers Park (Newgatestreet village) [1].6, *15*, *20*
    manor-house [10].9, 28
    OS grid ref. [10].32
Tolymer, John [4].16
Tolymer, Walter [1].20; [4].7
Tolymer, William [4].5, 16
Toogood, Joseph [11].27
Torrington, 5th Viscount, Diaries of [3].12, 27
Town and Country Planning [1].5
Town Centre [12].22
town houses [10].25-30
Town Lodge [8].5, 11
Townsend, Charles [8].11
Townsend, Elizabeth [3].24
trackway [4].5
Tractarians [7].21
trade [8].7
    regulation [6].5-6, 13
    tokens [3].15
trades [11].**11-40**
    analysis [11].**86-7**
    see also shops; *types of trades*

tradesmen: family pedigrees [11].42
Trade Unions [6].17
traffic [6].12; [8].25; [11].6
    Police Department [6].27
traffic lights [5].32
trains
    1900 [5].*24*
    diesel [5].23
    Lord Salisbury Special [5].23, *25*
    number per hour [5].26
    Silver Jubilee [5].27, *27*
    speed [5].21, 26-7
    Stirling Eight-Foot Singles [5].24, 25, *25*
    well tanks [5].23
    see also railways
trainspotters [5].28-9
transportation [6].17, 19, 21
travellers [11].43
Travellers' Lane [1].11; [2].*6*, *7*, *20*, *32*; [5].8, 16; [8].15, 32
Travellers Rest beer-house [3].*8*, 15, 31-2
trees
    early [2].4
    Roe Green ash [2].23
    at sanatorium [2].31
    sold, *1854* [9].*33*
    see also forest; oak trees; timber; woodland/woods
Tremhyde [9].6
trespassing [6].19
Triangle House [8].*30*, 31; [10].19-20, 28; [11].39, 83
    OS grid ref. [10].32
Trident aircraft [12].18
tripedresser [11].29
tripeman [11].87
triplets [7].10
troops [6].20
Trott (Trotte), Thomas [6].4, 7
Truck Act [5].13
Trussel, William [6].10
Tudor Revels [8].14-15

63

Tudor sovereigns [11].53
    see also names
Tukner, Henry [6].13
tunnels, railway [5].12, *17*, 26, 27
    Ponsbourne [4].*4*, 6, 25; [5].*17*
    Welwyn South [5].27-8
Turner, Arthur [4].12
Turner, John [6].6
Turner, Joseph [4].24
Turner, Mary [11].69
Turner, Mathew [4].22
turnips [9].17, 18, 19, 20, 21, 23, 42
    stealing [6].22
Turnpike Commissioners [11].6
Turnpike Road [2].*18*; [9].16
Turnpike Trust [1].11; [3].9, 12; [5].7-8
Turpin, Dick [3].28
Twenty Mile Bridge [12].9
Two Brewers pub [3].*8*, 19, 25, 32; [7].26; [11].*12*, 15
Two Wrestlers pub [3].20, 32
Tydder (Tidder), Cadwallader [11].53
Tydder (Tidder), Thomas [11].53, 54
Tydder, Fulk [11].53
Tydder, Onslow [11].53
Tyler family [11].62
    Tyler, Charlotte [8].20
    Tyler, Thomas [4].7
Tyler's Causeway [2].8; [3].31; [4].5, 7, 9, 23; [7].22; [12].15
Tyndall, John [1].3
typhoid [8].19

U

Uncle, Thomas [11].67
undertakers [11].39, 88
unemployment [9].26
Union Fire and Life Insurance Office [11].23
Union Lane *see* Wellfield Road

Union Workhouse [8].23-4
University of Hertfordshire [12].26
Union of Independents and Baptists [7].23
Upper Cromer Hyde [9].*24*
Upper Handside Farm [11].59
Upper Shot field strip [2].19
Upper Woodside [9].*24*
Urban District [12].11
Urwick, William
    Nonconformity in Herts [12].22
usher [11].88

V

V. A. D. Hospital [8].25; [12].7
vagrants [6].14-15
Valence family [4].8-10
    chart [4].*9*
Valentine family [11].54
Vallance, Thomas [6].17; [11].70
Valley Road
    1927 [12].*10*
    1955 [12].*10*
Vampire jet fighter [12].17
Vaughan family [11].53
    Vaughan, Cardinal Archbishop [7].27, 28
    Vaughan, Dr. Herbert [7].28
    Vaughan, Fr. Kenelm [7].27-8
Venables family [11].54
Venice [8].7, 8
Ventris, Michael [5].29
Veritys [2].32
Verulamium [1].25
Vestry Meeting [9].16
veterinary surgeon [11].88
viaducts
    Park Street [5].9; [11].7, 84
    Welwyn [5].11, 26, *27*
Vicarage
    Fore Street *see* Rectory (Vicarage), Fore Street
    Newgate Street [4].24
Victoria, Queen
    Golden Jubilee [8].18

visits Hatfield [7].8; [8].18; [12].26
death [12].5
Victoria County History [9].32
View of Frankpledge [6].4, 5
Vigors Croft [2].13, 32
Vigors, Mrs. [2].16, [9].44
vill [6].5
village green [4].24
violence [6].7
virgates [9].6, 7
Vixen (Wexen) Dell [2].21
voluntary groups [12].6-7, 15

W

Waby, Edward [11].31
Wackett, Abraham [4].23
Wackett, John [9].16
Wade, John [6].17
Wades, The [2].32
wages [10].6-7; [12].15-16
 farm [9].15, 17, 18, 23, 27, 36
Waggoners inn [3].13, 16, 23, 32
Walbee, Ann [11].32
Walby family [11].31-3, 39, 43, 54, 85
 pedigree [11].30
Walby, Benjamin [11].30
Walby, Edward [11].30, 32
Walby, Elizabeth [11].85
Walby, Ellen [11].30
Walby, George (d.1661) [11].30
Walby, George (d.1694) [11].30
Walby, George (d.1714) [11].30
Walby, George (d.1776) [11].30
Walby, George (d.1821) [11].30, 32, 33
Walby, George (d.1833) [11].30
Walby, George (d.1853) [11].30, 33, 84, 85
Walby, Henry William [11].26, 30, 33, 85
Walby, John [11].30, 32, 35
Walby, Joseph Canham [11].26, 30

Walby, Lydia [11].30, 31, 33, 35
Walby, Marcus John [11].30, 33
Walby, Martha [11].31-2, 35
Walby, William (d.1702) [11].30, 31, 39
Walby, William (d.1760) [11].30, 31
Walby, William (d.1764) [9].17; [11].30, 31
Walby, William (d.1770) [11].30, 31-2
Walby, William (d.1843) [9].27; [11].30, 32
Walby, William (d.1868) [11].85
Walby, William (d.1885) [11].26, 30
Walcroft [2].10
Walker family [9].44
 Walker, James [11].15
 Walker, Mrs. (schoolmistress) [8].23
Walkmerehyde [9].6
Wallars, Nuss [9].16
Waller, John [11].12, 27
Waller, William [11].27
Walshe, Elizabeth [6].8
Walter de Godarvill [4].6
Walter de Stoke [1].21; [2].8
Walter de Tolymer [1].22; [4].5, 6, 16
Walter of Henley [2].8
Walter the Smith [2].11, 24-5
Walter, Katherine [4].12
Waltraps (Walltraps; Waltrots; Waltrottes) Farm [2].5, 7, **11-13**, 14, 20, 24, 27; [9].7
 field names [2].19
 and law [6].7, 9
Waltraps Green [2].23
Waltrot, Thomas [2].5, 12; [6].4, 7
Wane, John Haynes [11].17
War Cry [5].19
War Memorial [12].7, 18
Ward, Albert [3].31

65

Ward, Ann [11].26
Ward, Ned
   The London Spies [2].27
Ware [4].12; [5].7
   malt-houses [3].5-6
Ware Park [7].29
Warren family [11].7, 19
   Warren, Thomas [11].65
Warren Farm [11].58
Warriner, Thomas [9].15
Warwick, John Dudley, 2nd Earl of
   [7].5; [8].16; [11].4
waste
   refuse [5].23
   woodland [9].7
watchmakers [11].67
water
   flooding [12].24
   WGC supplies [12].8, 9
   see also Rivers *and below*
watercress [9].48; [11].86
Water Dell (Waterdell) [2].21, *28*
Water End [9].41; [10].12-13
   OS grid ref. [10].32
Waterloo House [3].14; [11].22
Waters brothers [3].7, 14, 31
Waters family [11].43, 54, 73-4
   Waters, Edward [11].11
   Waters, F. N. [3].31
   Waters, Mr. (of Waters Garage)
   [2].14
   Waters, W. G. [3].14, 31
   Waters, Walter [11].74
Waters' Garage [1].10; [7].28
Waterships [9].6
water trough [8].16-17
Water Works [2].*6*
Watery Lane [2].*20*, 32
Watford [1].6; [9].40
   brewery [3].7; [11].59
   market [9].36
   Police [6].27
   railway [5].9, 18
wattle and daub [10].5
Watton at Stone [9].14

weather [8].24-5
weavers [11].39, 87
Webb family [11].61
   Webb, James [3].31; [11].43, 66
   Webb, James Simkins [11].14
   Webb, Mr. (in church, *19c.*) [7].8
   Webb, Sarah [3].24
   Webb, William [3].24; [8].11;
   [11].61
   Webb, William James [11].14, 61
Webster family [11].54
   Webster, G. H. [11].33
Welch, Patrick [11].69
Welham Green [2].22, *28*; [5].16;
   [7].29
Wellfield Old People's Home [1].7,
   7
Wellfield Road (Union Lane)
   [1].*14*; [2].31; [3].21,
   24, 31
Wellingham, George [11].29, 39
Wellingham, John [11].*12*, 39
Wellington, Arthur Wellesley, 1st
   Duke of [11].82
Wellington Field [9].27
Wells, Hardy [11].26
Wells, Richard Hardy [3].24
Welsh families [11].53
Welsh, James [11].10
Welwyn [4].19; [11].59
   church repair [5].6
   railway [5].11, 19, 21, 26
   tunnels [5].27-8
   viaduct [5].11, 26, *27*
Welwyn Builders [12].9, 15
Welwyn Foundry [12].15
Welwyn Garden City [12].3, **8-12**
   pre-war [1].4
   administration [12].11-13
   building [7].17; [12].9; [2].4
   buses [5].30
   churches [7].19-20, *map 20*
   employment [12].**14-16**
   farms [9].5, 6, 7, 41, 42, 45;
   [11].60

houses [1].4; [10].17, 29; [12].9-11
Hunters Bridge [5].13
New Town [1].5; [9].42; [12].19-22
Parish Council [11].60
population [5].4
pubs [3].21
railway [5].13, 23, 26
  accident [5].28
  station [5].16, 19, *20*, 21; [12].*4*, 15
schools [8].4
shops [12].11-12, 13
Urban District Council [11].60
Welwyn Junction [5].18
Welwyn-Luton railway [5].16
Welwyn Stores [12].12, 13
Welwyn Times [9].*14*
Wesley, Charles [7].25
Wesley, John [7].25
Wesleyan chapels and churches *see* Methodist and Wesleyan chapels and churches
West, Gilbert [11].35
West Goldings school [8].*30*, 32
West Ham, London [2].32
West Herts Infirmary [11].57
West Hyde [9].*24*, 29, 30, 32, 40
West Shot field strip [2].19
Westfield School [8].*30*, 31
Westminster Archdiocese [7].27
Westminster, Cardinal Archbishops of [7].29
  see also Bourne, Cardinal Archbishop; Hinsley, Cardinal; Vaughan, Cardinal Archbishop
Wetheringsete, Robert [7].*cover*
Wetherly, Francis [6].18-19
Wexendell [2].*7*, *20*, *28*
Whaley, John [7].22
wheat [9].17, 20, 21, 27, 47
Wheat Croft [2].36

Wheathampstead [1].6
  farms [9].14, 41; [11].57
Wheeler, Sir Mortimer [1].26
wheelwrights [11].*12*, 34, **35-6**, **71-4**, 86, 87
Whethampstead Springe [6].14
Whetstone [4].18
whipping post [6].7, *9*
Whitbread, Messrs. [3].29, 31, 32
Whitbread, Michael [7].22
Whitbread, Nathaniel [7].22
Whitby family [3].26
  Whitby, Abraham [11].42
  Whitby, Ann [11].42
  Whitby, Emma [11].42
  Whitby, G. [8].13
  Whitby, Josiah [3].26; [11].42
  Whitby, W. [8].12
White Hart [3].*17*, 27, 32
White Horse Field [9].13
White Horse Inn [3].*8*, 32; [10].21
White, John Hammond [11].61
White Lion (Lyon) inn, Fore Street *see* Salisbury Arms
White Lion pub, Newtown [3].8, *17*, 21
White Lion Square [1].7; [5].5; [8].32; [11].78; [12].21
White Lion, St. Albans Road [3].20, 32
White Swan, Stevenage [3].12
White, Mr. (of Roe Green South) [2].15, 17, 25, 31; [9].30
Whitehead, Litchfield [11].17
Whitelaw, W. [12].*4*
whitesmith [11].67
Whittard, Mr. (farmer) [9].29
Whittey, William [3].29
Whittimore, John [11].39
Whittingstall family [11].59
  Whittingstall, George [11].59
Wiches Farm [11].58
Wicks, John [11].14, 25
Wicks, Samuel [11].*12*, 14, 18

Wicks, Thomas [11].*12*, 25
Wild (Wild's) Hill (Wildhill [1].*6*,
   6, 21; [11].59, 71
   bridges [6].13
   cottages [10].16, 17, 20
   farms [9].6, *25*
   pub [3].25-6, 32
Wilde
   "The Changeling in the Pulpit"
      (poem) [7].11
Wildish, Mr. [7].26
Wilkins Green [2].22, *28*; [9].35
Wilkins Green Lane [10].30
   OS grid ref. [10].32
Wilkinson, Joseph [11].15, 19
Wilkinson, Richard [11].15, 79
Willetts, Richard [11].*12*
William III, German Emperor [8].18
William ad Collem [2].11, 24
William de Barra [1].22
William de Delle [2].24
William de Ludeford [11].62
William de Pomelsbourne [4].7
William de Ponsbourne [4].7
William de Shuneshull [6].10
William de Valence, Earl of
      Pembroke [4].8, 9
William de Wile [1].21
Williams, Fr. Percy Hemus [7].29
Willis family [2].10-11
   Willis, Edward, Bishop [2].10, 16
   Willis, John, Captain [2].16
wills [11].33, 53, 59
   1501 [11].59
   1661 [9].10-11
   1745 [11].38
   1785 [11].36
   1799 [11].33, 35
   1806 [11].37-8
   1822 [11].59
   of smallholders [9].10
Willsden House [10].28
   OS grid ref. [10].32
Willson, Mrs (licensee) [3].18
Willson family [11].54

Wilson family [11].43
   Wilson, Joseph [6].24
   Wilson, William [6].15
Winderich manor [4].10, 11, 12
windows [10].*26*, *27-8*
   tax [11].24
wine merchant [11].87
Wisman, Robin [6].13
Withy Mill [1].12, *13*; [2].25;
      [11].61
Wix, E. N. [8].28
Wolriche, William [7].5
woman's shop [11].19, 20-1
women
   hat-makers [2].30; [8].23;
      [11].87
   names [1].22
   Policewomen [6].27
   scolds [6].27
   V.A.D.s [8].25; [12].7
   voluntary work [12].6
   see also school mistresses
wood *see* timber
wood-block paving [5].8
Woodfield farm [1].*15*; [4].21;
      [11].78
Woodger, William [7].21
Wood Green: railway [5].19, 23, 26,
      27
Wood Hall [4].*26*
   farms [9].6, 23, 30, 33
Woodhall [3].19; [9].7; [11].76;
      [12].9, 12
   cottage [10].12-13, *13*
   OS grid ref. [10].32
Woodhall Lodge Farm [9].*24*, 32;
      [11].61
   service conducted at [7].16
Woodhall Manor [1].22
   manor-house [10].9
Woodhill [8].24; [9].*25*, 31, 46
   church [7].15, 16, 21
   school [8].31
Woodhill House [1].*15*
Woodhouse, Mary Ann [11].16

woodland/woods [2].4, 10; [6].14;
  [9].6-7, 9, 30, 33
  see also forest; Great Wood
Woodman pub, Hatfield Hyde
  [3].*16*, 21, 23, 25, 32
Woodman, Wild Hill [3].25-6, 32
wood merchant [11].42
Woodright [10].5
Woods Avenue [2].*6*, 32; [7].27, 29
Woods Avenue Protest Group
  [12].26
Woodside (Bokenhamhide ,
    Bokymwykhide,
    Buckhamwykhyde,
    Bukhamwik,
    Bukhamwyk, Wood
    Side, Woodsyde) [1].6,
    8, 11, *15*, 21, *21*, 25;
    [2].*28*; [7].11; [11].37,
    40, 59, 74, 76, 81
  constables [6].20
  cottages [10].23, *24*
    OS grid ref. [10].32
  farms [9].6, **26-8**, 29, 30, 31, 32,
    46, 47
  Gate to Hatfield Park [1].9
  inn [3].12, 30
  Lower Woodside
    farm [1].15; [9].9, *24*, 44
    hamlet [1].13
  North Road [3].9
  Police [6].20
  postal services [11].78
  potters [11].63
  tithing group [6].5
  Upper Woodside [9].24
  village pound [6].7
Woodside Green [5].8
Woodside Place [1].*13*; [11].75, *75*,
  76
Woodward family [3].29
  Woodward, C. R. [8].32
wool [6].11; [9].17; [11].39
Woolaston, Richard [4].13
Woolmer Green [5].12, 27

Woolwich prison hulks [6].17
Worbiss, John [3].29
Workhouse (Work House) [1].7, *7*;
  [7].14; [9].46
  Union, children in [8].23-4
World War I [11].45; [12].7
  Brewery [3].7
  casualties [3].7; [11].76
  farms [9].37, 41
  housing [10].29
  ministers [7].24
  and railway [4].6, 25
  Roe Green [2].31
  and schools [8].25
  timber [9].7
World War II [10].30; [12].**17, 18**
  bomb damage [6].26; [8].15;
    [12].17
  and churches [7].19, 20, 25
  and farms [2].17; [9].47, 48
  Newgate Street [4].6, 26
  Police work [6].26
  and railway [4].6
  and schools [8].15, 25-6
World's End [2].*28*
Worlibank [11].64
Worman, Herbert [8].23
Wormley [4].13
Wray, Martha [11].71
Wren family [11].54
Wrestlers pub [1].11; [3].*16*, 20, 23,
  32; [5].15
Wright, George [2].12
Wright, Thomas [6].5
Wright, William [6].21; [11].5-6
Wyle, John and William de la [9].6

Y

Yearly, Thomas [11].63
yokes [2].8
York [5].*11*, 14
  Railway Museum [5].25
York Waggon [5].8
Yorke, F. R. S. [10].30

Young, Arthur [2].21; [9].18, 42
   A General View of the
      Agriculture of
      Hertfordshire [2].21;
   [9].18-19, 20, 21, 22, 23
Young, Benjamin [3].7, 21, 29, 30;
   [7].23; [11].25, 43
Young, John [3].5
Young, Miss (publican) [3].30

Young, Mr. (farmer) [9].20, 21
Young, Robert [7].22, 23
Younge, Margaret [6].13

Z

Zenzano, Annibali (Hannibal
   Zenzan; Hennyball
   Zinzan) [1].17, 18
Zvegintseff, Alexander L. [8].18

www.ingramcontent.com/pod-product-compliance
Lightning Source LLC
Chambersburg PA
CBHW071412040426
42444CB00009B/2220